# MYSTERIOUS WAYS

# MYSTERIOUS WAYS

### The Providence of God

### in the Life of Joseph

David Kingdon

THE BANNER OF TRUTH TRUST

# THE BANNER OF TRUTH TRUST

*Head Office*
3 Murrayfield Road
Edinburgh
EH12 6EL, UK

*North America Office*
PO Box 621
Carlisle
PA 17013, USA

banneroftruth.org

First published 2004
© Banner of Truth Trust 2004
Reprinted 2020, 2021 (special)

\*

ISBN: 978 0 85151 871 0

\*

Typeset in 12/15 Goudy Old Style BT
at The Banner of Truth Trust, Edinburgh

Printed in the USA by
Versa Press Inc.,
East Peoria, IL.

Unless otherwise indicated, Scripture quotations are from
THE HOLY BIBLE, NEW INTERNATIONAL VERSION,
© 1978, International Bible Society.

# Contents

# Foreword

When I first read the manuscript of this splendid new book by David Kingdon I was transported back in time to childhood days, when, with few books in our house, I discovered my grandmother's thick, leather-bound (but amazingly small-print!) Bible.

I suppose I was probably only five years old, a beginning but extremely enthusiastic reader. On cold winter mornings, before the days of central heating, I would slip into my parents' recently vacated bed, snuggle under the warm covers and try to find one or other of my two favourite stories in Grandmother's Book. Daniel was terrific, but difficult to find, because he was hidden among strange sounding names more than half-way through the book! But Joseph was almost impossible to find because he had no book named after him! Yet once found, in imagination I would be transported back to the world of special robes, family jealousies, dangerous experiences, but courageous faithfulness to God; back to a world of danger, temptation, jail, dreams, disappointment – but eventually to Pharaoh's palace, to clever plans and to family reunion.

Joseph was great. He was God's man. Indeed it was difficult to decide between him and Daniel for the title of greatest human hero. The Lone Ranger, Superman, Dan Dare could never compete with Joseph!

In early teenage years I would need the lessons that were then being taught me. For my parents did not then attend church, and, like Joseph, I often felt far away from them, spiritually in another world, and longed for God's blessing in my family, so that we would all be together in God's grace. God seemed so slow, and I felt so small, and prayers seemed to go unheard. It is easier now, looking back, to see that God's calendar and ours are not the same.

Most of us find ourselves there at some point in our lives – in some cases at many points. How can we rest in the assurance that 'God is on the field when he is most invisible'? How can we follow the path of the Lord when, as William Cowper reminds us, 'He plants his footsteps in the sea', where no footprints can be seen, or believe He smiles when all we see is a 'frowning providence'?

As Isaiah notes, the children of light sometimes find themselves walking in darkness (*Isa.* 50:10). That is why David Kingdon's exposition of the story of Joseph can be a significant help to us. In reading these pages, we find ourselves in a 'safe pair of hands' to help guide us and point out to us the great lessons we need to learn and re-learn. For in David Kingdon we find great skill in exposition, written in the spirit of someone who (although he does not allude to it) has lifelong personal experience of dark and difficult providences. We are assured that God works everything together for the good of those who love him. This book itself is testimony to that. Its publication is itself an expression of God's good providence in the life of its author, making him someone who combines the ability to understand the text of Scripture with the sensitive heart of a pastor who has been well prepared to be our friend and guide in this area of spiritual experience.

This is not a long book, nor should it be. I am sure that you will find, as I have done, that its value is much greater than its size. Enjoy it, benefit from it, turn to it again and again, make the truths it teaches your own. And then pass them (and perhaps the book too!) on to others.

SINCLAIR B. FERGUSON
Westminster Theological Seminary
Dallas, Texas
May 2004

# Preface

With the exception of Chapter Seven, the sermons on which this book is based were preached to the congregation of Mount Zion English Baptist Church in Cardigan, West Wales, during July and August 1981.

My aim in the series, as in this book, was strictly pastoral – to help believers to better understand the doctrine of God's providence, and to live experimentally in its light each day of their lives.

The life of Joseph is, I believe, recorded in Holy Scripture so that we may draw from it much insight into the workings of God's providence. From the biblical narrative I have sought to draw out its twists and turns, its hiddenness and mystery, and its place in the unfolding of God's covenant purposes.

I have deliberately kept the language of the book simple and the paragraphs short in the hope that this little book will be read easily by believers whose first language is not English.

My thanks are due to my wife Susan who has word-processed most of my hand-written script (not always easy to read!) with skill and patience.

This book is dedicated to the three churches in which it has been my privilege to expound the Word of God (see the Dedication on page v). The gaps between pastorates, in case readers should wonder, are due to God's ordering in His providence other tasks for me to undertake, first as Principal of the Irish Baptist College, Belfast (1963–74) and then as Theological Books Editor at Inter Varsity Press (UK) from 1984 to 1993 and Managing Editor of the Bryntirion Press of the Evangelical Movement of Wales (1996–99).

My prayer is that these chapters will help and comfort many a tried and tested Christian. If I have learned anything during my Christian pilgrimage of over fifty years, it can be summed up in this exhortation from William Cowper (1731–1800) in his great hymn, 'GOD MOVES IN A MYSTERIOUS WAY':

> *Judge not the Lord by feeble sense,*
> *But trust Him for His grace;*
> *Behind a frowning providence*
> *He hides a smiling face.*

DAVID KINGDON
April 2004

# 1

# The Big Picture

We are going to look at the life of Joseph, as it is recorded in Genesis. If there is one biblical doctrine that is highlighted by his life, it is the doctrine of the providence of God. When we consider this doctrine we can approach it along the line of Systematic Theology, as the *Westminster Confession of Faith* does, for example. That is to say, we can frame a definition of providence by bringing together texts drawn from various parts of Scripture. So in the *Confession* we read:

> God, the great Creator of all things, doth uphold, direct, dispose, and govern all creatures, actions and things, from the greatest even to the least, by his most wise and holy providence, according to his infallible fore-knowledge, and the free and immutable counsel of his own will, to the praise of the glory of his wisdom, power, justice, goodness, and mercy.
>
> [Chapter 5: *Of Providence*, Section 1]

This approach to the doctrine has the great value of enabling us to see it as a whole.

However, I suspect that most of us find it easier to grasp a doctrine experimentally as we see it worked out in the life of a biblical character. So as we look at the life of Joseph one result will be, I trust, that we have a better understanding of the providence of God – and not just a better understanding but a deep heart-appreciation of it as well, so that we learn to live in it day by day.

We are introduced to Joseph at Genesis 37:2. His story – with certain interludes – runs to the end of Genesis (50:26). He was born in Canaan to Rachel, the favourite wife of Jacob (Gen. 30:22–24). But he spent the greater part of his life in Egypt, first as a slave, then as a prisoner, and finally as a royal official next in importance to the Pharaoh himself.

How did Joseph come to be in Egypt? Well, one answer is that his brothers sold him to some Midianite merchantmen who took him to Egypt and sold him in turn to Potiphar, a captain of Pharaoh's guard (Gen. 37:28–36). But equally true (and in no way in opposition to this first answer), is that God in his providence so ordered the life of Joseph that he was taken to Egypt to fulfil the promise that God would make of Abram's descendants a great nation (12: 2). Thus, in the life of Joseph, we see an interweaving of the sinful acts of men with the sovereign will of God, so that they, in spite of themselves and with no thought of God, in fact carried out his will. Joseph himself twice confesses as much (Gen. 45:7–8; 50:20).

We must therefore begin our study by looking at the life of Joseph against the background of the sovereign purpose of God as expressed in his covenant promise. For unless we do so we shall miss a whole dimension of the life of Joseph, and we shall accordingly fail to appreciate how marvellous are the ways of our God.

## 1. THE PROMISE GOD MADE

When God called the first patriarch Abram, later renamed Abraham, in the land of the Chaldees, in the city of Ur, he promised that he would make of him a great nation. Not just a great clan, nor a great tribe, but far more – a great nation (*Gen.* 12:2)!

Yet his wife, Sarai, was barren (*Gen.* 11:30). Then, after many years of waiting, in which faith was sorely tried, Isaac was born. Both parents were well past the age at which they could expect a child to be born to them. But even before Isaac was born, and the wheels were, so to speak, set in motion whereby a great nation should issue from father Abraham, God gave to the patriarch a most remarkable revelation of the future.

His descendants were to be strangers in a land that was not theirs (*Gen.* 15:13). There they were to be oppressed and obliged to serve as slaves for four hundred years. But in the fourth generation (one patriarchal generation appears to be a hundred years) they would return to the land of Canaan.

During these long, hard years in Egypt the numbers of Israel would multiply greatly. Seventy persons would enter Egypt (*Gen.* 46:27) – a mere clan. Yet from Egypt would come forth a great nation, because the children of Israel would have multiplied exceedingly (*Exod.* 1:7,12).

Now how did they come to be in Egypt? Why was it that they left the land of Canaan? It was because, in a time of famine in Canaan, Joseph, the brother who had been sold into Egypt, occupied a position that he could use to support his family (*Gen.* 45:7–8; 50:20).

Of course, when Joseph was sold into Egypt – when he was a slave in Potiphar's household – he would have had no idea that he was being used to fulfil God's long-range purpose of making Israel a great nation. Had he judged the Lord simply by what he had permitted to happen to him, he would have sadly misjudged his God. From being his father's favourite son he became a slave. Being unjustly accused by a wicked woman, he had been thrown into prison. And there he was, left to languish even when he had helped the chief butler (Pharaoh's cup-bearer) to escape from it by interpreting his dream.

How easy it would have been for Joseph to have concluded that God had no good purpose for his life. Surely the hand of God was against him! Evil had befallen him! How easy it would have been for Joseph to rebel against God, to cry out in anger against him! And how easy it is for us to do the same, to look at the evil, grim events of our lives and to conclude that God is against us! But we must never forget:

> *Behind a frowning providence*
> *He hides a smiling face.*
> William Cowper

We must learn not to isolate one event, or even a series of events, from the rest of our lives. We must try to see God's overall purpose – to get the big picture. This is what Joseph did. He recognized the evil done to him but he did not doubt the over-ruling purpose of God. He confessed to his brothers: 'But as for you, ye thought evil against me; but God meant it unto good, to bring to pass, as it is this day, to save much people alive' (*Gen.* 50:20, AV).

God had made a promise, and its fulfilment hinged upon Joseph being sold into Egypt as a slave. To fulfil his purpose God used the sinful act of Joseph's brothers without in any way condoning it. So never let us assume that he will only permit what is good and pleasant to befall us. This is often what we do when we reproach God for allowing evil events to happen to us.

## 2. THE UNFOLDING OF THE STORY (GENESIS 37:1–28)

The story of Joseph is a very human one. It rings true because it is so close to life, with its themes of favouritism provoking hatred, and the pampered son making matters worse.

The story revolves around the fact that *Joseph was the favourite son of his father* (Gen. 37:3). He was the son of Rachel, Jacob's favourite wife (Gen. 30:23–24), as was Benjamin (Gen. 35:16–18), whereas the brothers who came to hate Joseph were his half-brothers, 'the sons of Bilhah and the sons of Zilpah' (Gen. 37:2), the slave-wives of Jacob. Chapter thirty-four has already shown that there was little love lost between Jacob and the sons of Leah (Gen. 34:30, 31). It seems highly likely that Jacob had even less affection for his sons by Bilhah and Zilpah.

Jacob made no attempt to conceal his love for Joseph. It stemmed from the fact that 'he had been born to him in his old age' (Gen. 37:3) and he doted upon him in consequence. Had he been wiser, Jacob would have tried to hide his deep love for Joseph from his brothers and to treat them as equally as possible. Instead he almost flaunted his love for his favourite son by making 'a richly ornamented robe for him'. Whatever is the meaning of the Hebrew expression it is clear that this garment sent a very definite signal to Joseph's brothers: 'When his brothers saw that their father loved him more than any of them, they hated him and could not speak a kind word to him' (verse 4).

So another element is added to the unfolding story: *Joseph was hated by his brothers* (verse 4). They envied him because of the place that he had in their father's affections, and envy led to hatred and hatred to harsh words.

Nor did Joseph himself try to pour oil on troubled waters, rather the reverse, for *by his foolishness he made the situation worse* (verses 5–11). He had a prophetic dream and, instead of keeping it to himself, 'he told it to his brothers'. As a result 'they hated him all the more'. If his brothers might have been unclear about the meaning of the dream Joseph was in no doubt about its import. He made it very plain to them. 'He said to them, "Listen to this dream I had: We were binding sheaves of grain out in the field when suddenly my sheaf rose and stood upright, while your sheaves gathered around mine and bowed down to it"'(verse 7).

Their reaction to the foolish talk of their teenage brother was entirely predictable. 'They hated him all the more because of his dream and what he had said' (verse 8).

Joseph had a second dream, a dream that was more extravagant than the first. In it the sun and moon and eleven stars bowed down to him. Joseph took no notice of his brothers' reaction to his first dream. It would have been wise if he had kept the content of his second dream to himself, but it seems that he simply had to blurt it out!

When Joseph told the second dream to his father he received a strong rebuke, but whether he was suitably chastened we are not told. Given his previous insensitivity, it is unlikely that he was.

We can learn some instructive lessons from this story. First, Jacob was wrong to have a favourite son. And he was even more wrong to single him out in the way that he did, making him so evidently his personal favourite.

[6]

Parents need to be wise – to treat their children equally because they love them equally. And if there is a favourite child, for some children are more likeable than others, they ought not to show favour.

Second, Joseph was wrong, for by his foolish parading of his dreams he simply rubbed salt into his brothers' wounds.

Lastly, Joseph's brothers were wrong to hate Joseph. He could not help being his father's favourite son. It was not right for them to take it out on Joseph because they envied him.

Children who feel that they are not favourites ought not to give way to envy, for envy leads to hatred, and hatred to murder, or at least, in the case of Joseph's brothers, to a determination to get Joseph out of their lives.

The last part of the story – the selling of Joseph into slavery – is told at some length (verses 12–36). As a semi-nomadic clan with numerous sheep and cattle to feed, Joseph's brothers were obliged to seek new grazing grounds at fairly regular intervals. At first they grazed their animals near Shechem, between Mount Ebal and Mount Gerizim (verse 13). But when Joseph arrived there at his father's bidding he found that they had moved on to new pastures (verses 15–17). Eventually he caught up with them at Dothan, a settlement about twenty-five miles north of Shechem.

The narrator emphasizes the intense hatred of Joseph's brothers. When they saw him in the distance 'they plotted to kill him' (verse 18). The next verse underlines the sheer venom that filled their hearts. '"Here comes that dreamer!" they said to each other. "Come now, let's kill him and throw him into this cistern here in the desert and say that a ferocious animal devoured him. Then we'll see what comes of his dreams"'. Not all the brothers were prepared to go so far as this, for Reuben formed a plan to rescue him (verses 21–22). Judah also wanted to save Joseph's life and did so when the rest of his brothers accepted his suggestion that he be sold to passing Midianite merchants (verses 26–29). But all the brothers were guilty of deceiving their father for years by pretending that a wild animal had killed Joseph (verses 31–35).

Joseph had left his home a free man, but he became a slave in Egypt in the house of Potiphar, 'one of Pharaoh's officials, the captain of the guard' (verse 36). What a radical change in his circumstances! From a pampered favourite son to a humble slave!

What can we learn about God's providence from this story? And how can we profit from what we learn?

In the first place we see that *when God uses evil men to accomplish his purposes he is not obliged to justify himself to anyone.* Joseph's brothers knew that they wanted to get rid of the brother they hated. They thought only in terms of their hatred. What they did not know is that they were serving a deep purpose of God – 'the saving of many lives' (50: 20).

Joseph too did not know why God had permitted him to be sold into slavery in Egypt. God did not tell him. Only in the light of later events would Joseph be able to say to his brothers, 'But as for you, you meant evil against me; but God meant it for good' (*Gen.* 50:20, NKJV).

The God of the Bible is not obliged to justify his ways to us. This is a truth that we find hard to accept. When our world is turned upside down, as Joseph's was, we so often demand to know the reason why. God's ways are always right, but he is not obliged to explain them to us.

This is Paul's argument when he considers God's *freedom* in the choosing of his people. 'But who are you, O man, to talk back to God? Shall what is formed say to him who formed it, "Why did you make me like this?" [see Isaiah 29:6; 45:9]. Does not the potter have the right to make out of the same lump of clay some pottery for noble purposes and some for common use?' (*Rom.* 9: 20–21).

We may sometimes be baffled by the twists and turns of God's providence. When we are, we must learn to 'trust where we cannot trace' and to worship God instead of bombarding him with questions that He, for reasons known to Him, does not choose to answer immediately we ask them. The apostle Paul shows us the way forward in Romans 11:33:

> Oh, the depth of the riches of the wisdom
> and knowledge of God!
> How unsearchable his judgments,
> and his paths beyond tracing out!

In the light of this doxology it is surely wise to trust God and to wait for his purpose to be made known to us.

In the second place we learn that *there is sometimes a great gap in time between the tragedy that God permits and the good he plans to bring forth from it.* It was years after he was sold into Egypt that Joseph was raised to a position of great power and influence. And it was years later still when there was a widespread famine and, because of Joseph's foresight, there was food in Egypt when his family in Canaan needed it.

We know that 'in all things God works for the good of those who love him, who have been called according to his purpose' (*Rom.* 8: 28) – but not all at once! Yet we in our haste, and because we make our comfort the great consideration, often demand that good immediately flow from evil. But God does not work to our timetable, or to our demands.

He is sovereign, and He is free to do as he pleases for his glory. If king Nebuchadnezzar could accept this truth surely we can accept it as well. 'He does as he pleases with the powers of heaven and the peoples of the earth. No one can hold back his hand or say to him: "What have you done?"' (*Dan.* 4: 35).

So we must learn to submit to God's wisdom and His power. When faced with the inscrutability of His providence we must not put God in the dock and subject him to cross-examination. We must take William Cowper's words to heart:

> *Deep in unfathomable mines*
> *Of never-failing skill,*
> *He treasures up his bright designs,*
> *And works his sovereign will.*

So learn experimentally to rest in God. Doubt your own wisdom, rather than question His. And if on earth we are not given to know the reason God has permitted something to befall us, let us realize that God has all the years of eternity to tell us why.

# 2

# From Potiphar's House
# to Pharaoh's Prison

On one level of explanation Joseph, as we saw in the previous chapter, came to be in Egypt because, out of envy and a desire to be rid of him, his brothers sold him into slavery. But on another level of explanation, Joseph came to be in Egypt because God in His providence ordered it so. Through the hatred of his brothers God was to work His purpose – to preserve his chosen people, still a clan (*Gen.* 46:26–27) rather than a nation (see *Gen.* 12:2; *Exod.* 1:7), from starvation.

So in the life of Joseph we see an interweaving of the sinful attitudes of envy, hatred and deceit, with the sovereign will of God. In spite of themselves, and with no thought of God in what they did when they sold him into slavery, Joseph's brothers were carrying out God's will. And Joseph himself much later was able to confess that this was so (*Gen.* 50:20).

Ultimately Joseph came to be in Egypt because God had a promise to fulfil, the one he had made to Abram when he called him in Ur of the Chaldees. This promise, that he would make childless Abram into 'a great nation' (*Gen.* 12:2), was made good as the Israelites so multiplied in numbers in fertile Goshen (*Gen.* 47:27) that they came to be seen as a threat to the stability of the Egyptian state (*Exod.* 1:6–10).

The growth of the clan of Jacob into the nation of the Israelites was itself a stage in the future implementation of another element in the original promises made to Abram. Before the land of Canaan could be possessed by the seed of Abraham (*Gen.* 12:7), Israel had to become a nation capable, with God's help, of conquering and settling it. A mere clan could not have possessed the land – only a nation could do so. Thus the settlement of a clan in Egypt not only saved its members from starvation; it also began the next stage in the unfolding of God's purpose. The way to possess Canaan lay through the land of Egypt.

Joseph did not live to see the great growth in numbers of his people nor the oppression they suffered, but he was the vital link between their preservation and their possession of the land of Canaan.

As we take up his story again in this chapter (Genesis 39) we see Joseph placed by God's providence in two widely contrasting places – the house of Potiphar (verses 1–19), and then the prison-house of Pharaoh (verses 20–23). Of both places, the one as congenial to Joseph as the other was unpleasant, it is said significantly, 'the LORD was with him' (verses 3 and 21).

## 1. POTIPHAR'S HOUSE

The country in which Joseph now lived and the place of his abode were not of his choosing. He was a slave in the household of Potiphar, the captain of Pharaoh's guard (verse 1). No longer a pampered favourite son, Joseph must now serve others. Yet God is with him (verse 2), the living Presence which sweetens his situation.

As you read these pages you too may be in a situation that is not of your choosing. God, could you but realize it, has put you where you are for a purpose. But you are rebelling against your circumstances. Like the psalmist you long for the wings of a dove so that you can fly away and be at rest (*Psa.* 55: 6). Yet God does not satisfy your desire to escape. You need to recognize that He never puts his servants where He is not. As He was with Joseph, so He is with you. Enjoy His presence in your immediate circumstances, and forsake the folly of rebelling against God's providence. The way of wisdom lies in accepting God's providence, not in kicking against it.

In the house of Potiphar, Joseph *came to occupy a position of trust* (verses 3–6). Potiphar saw that the Lord was with Joseph and that he gave him success in all that he did (verse 3). This does not mean that Potiphar knew God, but that he concluded from Joseph's success that his (Joseph's) god was with him. Potiphar was attracted to Joseph as a man of ability and integrity. So Joseph found favour in his master's eyes (verse 4) and he made him his right hand man – his overseer (AV) or attendant (NIV).

Potiphar placed a great deal of trust in Joseph. He put him in charge of all his affairs, both inside and outside his house (verse 5). The only area of responsibility from which he excluded Joseph was that of his table, 'the food he ate'. This may have been because a non-Egyptian like Joseph would not have been allowed to take part in certain rituals connected with food. A more prosaic reason may have been that Potiphar liked to draw up his own menus!

[13]

As the manager of Potiphar's estate, Joseph would undoubtedly learn Egyptian methods of administration. He would have become familiar with land management practices and Egyptian principles of accounting. It is also likely that he would have gained a knowledge of Egyptian law. So, in a place which he would never have chosen, Joseph was being prepared, all unknown to himself, for the time when he would administer the whole of Egypt.

It was no accident that Joseph was sold as a slave to such a prominent person as Potiphar. Nor was it by chance that Potiphar entrusted him with the administration of his affairs. Though Joseph did not know it, his time in Potiphar's household was a period of preparation for yet greater responsibility as Pharaoh's second-in-command (*Gen.* 41:43). God was not only with Joseph; He was also preparing Joseph for future usefulness to his own people.

God makes no mistakes. Even when our situation may be far from our liking, when perhaps we would far rather be back home with our loved ones, God is at work preparing us for some future task. If we are not careful we can be so busy complaining about our circumstances, or even so prostrated by depression because we cannot escape from them, that we have no eye to see what God is doing in our lives.

William Cowper wisely warns us against this common mistake:

> *Judge not the Lord by feeble sense,*
> *But trust him for his grace;*
> *Behind a frowning providence*
> *He hides a smiling face.*

Though Joseph came to occupy a position of trust Potiphar's house also proved to be *a place of temptation* (verses

7b–18). Joseph was young. He was well-built and handsome. It was not long before he attracted the amorous attention of Potiphar's wife.

We know from contemporary records that the morals of Egyptian women were notoriously lax. So, not surprisingly, Potiphar's wife sets out to seduce Joseph (verse 7). No doubt to her astonishment her advances meet with a blank refusal. Joseph will not give in to her blandishments for two reasons. In the first place he makes it clear that he will not betray his master's trust. 'Everything he owns he has entrusted to my care' (verse 8), says Joseph. 'But you are the exception. You are *his* wife, not mine. So I am not free to go to bed with you, nor', he could have added, 'are you free to go to bed with me.'

What Potiphar's wife was asking him to do – make love to her – is unthinkable. Joseph will not betray his master's trust, nor his kindness, with unfaithfulness. For him the marriage bond is sacred. Even though the woman persisted with her advances, keeping up the pressure on Joseph day by day (verse 10), he steadfastly refused her and as much as possible kept out of her way. Perhaps it was such situations that Paul had in mind when he urged Timothy to 'flee the evil desires of youth, and pursue righteousness' (2 *Tim.* 2:22).

Joseph refused the advances of Potiphar's wanton wife for another reason. What she was proposing would have involved not only broken trust but also sinning against God (verse 9). She did not see that what she asked of Joseph was wrong, but for him it was wicked, a sin against God.

It is clear from Joseph's response that he is moved by the fear of God. He will not break His law and offend Him. So, at the risk of offending Potiphar's wife, he point blank refuses her advances. Joseph will not sin against God even if, as proved to be the case, loyalty to God means injustice for him.

[15]

What is striking is how vital the fear of God is in Joseph's life. It is so essential, so immediately present to his consciousness, that his reaction to what Potiphar's wife wanted was almost instinctive. 'How then could I do such a wicked thing and sin against God?' (verse 9). Joseph expects the answer to be clear to the woman because it is absolutely clear to him. His fear of God rules out a visit to her bed, now and always.

When I was a young Christian, over fifty years ago, it was quite common to hear a believer described as a God-fearing man or woman. Yet today I never hear such a thing said of any believer. The reason, it seems to me, is because the fear of God has dropped out of Christian vocabulary – it is a forgotten concept. Indeed I have even been told that it has no place in the New Testament, which commands us to love God and not to fear Him. (This in spite of such verses as Acts 5:11; 9:31; 2 Corinthians 7:1).

The fear of God was a vital principle of Joseph's conduct. He walked in the fear of the Lord, so that when powerful temptation presented itself he refused to respond. He did not take into account the consequences of rejecting the advances of a formidable woman. Neither did he ask as a modern liberal Christian like Joseph Fletcher, the proponent of 'situation ethics', would have done in Joseph's position, 'What would love have me do in this situation?' The biblical Joseph engaged in no such sophistry. His answer was so clear because the fear of God was so real.

Again and again, the book of Proverbs makes clear the connection between walking in the fear of God and true morality. 'To fear the LORD is to hate evil' (*Prov.* 8:13). There is an implacable antithesis, which allows no room for compromise, between fearing God and hating evil as *God,* not man, defines it. And when there is a vital fear of God in the believer's heart there is an adverse reaction to evil. In the robust language of the Authorized Version, 'By the fear of the LORD men depart from evil' (*Prov.* 16: 6).

Has the fear of God a place in your life? Is it in your heart as a vital principle that regulates your conduct? Does the fear of God enable you to rebuff temptation, especially strong, persistent temptation that seductively holds out the prospect of pleasure should you respond to it? Don't dally with temptation. Don't reason with it. Flee from it, for godliness has a negative side to it that we too often forget today. Many a sad fall would have been avoided if a living fear of God had ruled in the lives of professing Christians.

Joseph lived aware that God saw his every action. Potiphar might have been absent from the house but God was there, and Joseph knew it. The father's warning words to his son against the wiles of an adulteress apply very aptly to Joseph:

Why be captivated, my son, by an adulteress?
Why embrace the bosom of another man's wife?
For a man's ways are in full view of the LORD,
And he examines all his paths (*Prov.* 5:20–21).

Joseph's success in resisting temptation is not the end of the story. Potiphar's wife, having constantly met with refusal, now turned against Joseph and cleverly schemed her revenge. One day when his duties took him into the house from which all the servants were absent (verse 11) Joseph was again approached by her. This time, however, she grabbed his cloak and held onto it when he ran out of the house (verse 12).

Calling to her servants she falsely accused him of attempting to rape her (verse 14) and she waved his under-garment before them as proof of his evil intention. When her husband came home she repeated her 'story' to him to such effect that 'he burned with anger' (verse 19) and had Joseph consigned to prison. But not any prison, as we shall see, for it was 'the place where the king's prisoners were confined' (verse 20).

Joseph rightly resisted temptation, but *his virtue went unrewarded.* Instead of being commended by Potiphar, who seems to have listened only to his wife's lies, Joseph was 'rewarded' by being put in prison. What happened to him gives the lie to the superficial idea that virtue will always be swiftly rewarded. Though it sometimes passes for orthodoxy, this idea has no support in Scripture, as the fate of the Lord Jesus shows. Our Saviour was without sin. He went about doing good. Yet He was 'rewarded' with the cross (*1 Pet.* 2: 21–24).

He was the truly innocent sufferer, denied justice by the courts of men, but vindicated by His Father when He raised him from the dead. In His innocent suffering the Lord Jesus has left us an example (*1 Pet.* 2:21) of how we should behave as Christians (*1 Pet.* 4:16) when we experience 'the pain of unjust suffering' (*1 Pet.* 2:19). Our calling is to do what is right in God's sight and to leave our ultimate vindication to Him. He will see us right, even if we have to wait until the last judgment (see Romans 12:19).

## 2. PHARAOH'S PRISON

From Potiphar's house Joseph goes to Pharaoh's prison. An honoured slave, he is now branded as a would-be rapist who has betrayed his master's trust. Seeking only to please God, he has angered Potiphar and received injustice.

The sudden reversal of Joseph's future must have been a tremendous shock to him and a real test of his faith. For

Joseph, as for many of God's children through the centuries, providence does not take an even course. It has many twists and turns in it, some very sudden and surprising indeed. At times, change comes so suddenly, so seemingly out of any relation to what has gone before, that we are baffled. Then the agonized cry arises in our hearts, even if if does not escape our lips, 'Why has this happened to me? What have I done to deserve this?'

The answer may well be, 'Absolutely nothing.' You no more deserve what may be afflicting you now than Joseph did when he was unjustly thrown into prison. God did not tell Joseph why he was in prison even though the Lord had a purpose in his being there. For reasons best known to Himself God seldom reveals to His servants in advance what His providential purpose is. He expects us to trust Him, to take what we know of His revealed character as righteous and faithful, and to let that be our guide when life seems more of a maze than a straight path to heaven. This was the position Job took by faith when in the furnace of undeserved affliction he confessed, 'Though he slay me, yet will I trust in him' (*Job* 13:15, AV).

Whether Joseph questioned God, we are not told. He may have done, but Scripture is silent as to whether he did or did not. What is clear is that God was with him (verse 21). The presence of the Lord with us is more important than knowing what God's purpose for us is. To an infant the presence of parents is much more needful than to know what their plans for his future life are. John Wesley grasped this when he was dying. As the forty-sixth Psalm was being read to him, though he was extremely weak, he raised himself up from his bed and exclaimed, 'Best of all is, God is with us' (see Psalm 46, verses 7 and 11).

And the covenant kindness of God (verse 20) towards Joseph in prison is much more important than knowing in advance what His purpose is in allowing him to be there. For as in the house of Potiphar, so now in Pharaoh's prison, God granted Joseph favour in the eyes of the prison warden. He, like Potiphar, put Joseph in a position of trust and delegated to him many responsibilities. These included looking after important prisoners, as we shall see in the next chapter.

The house of Potiphar led to Pharaoh's prison, 'the place where the king's prisoners were confined.' (verse 20). Though Joseph did not know it then, *the way to his place at Pharaoh's side lay from Potiphar's house through Pharaoh's prison.*

God's providence has strange twists and turns to it. It may seem that, as with Joseph, He permits us to go from bad to worse. To be a slave is bad enough, but to be a prisoner is much worse. Yet it is the prisoner who becomes the man next in importance to Pharaoh. It is the hated brother who will use his position to save not only his brothers but the rest of his clan as well. And looking back he will see the hand of God at work in every twist and turn of the way. He will be able to say to the very ones who sold him into slavery, 'But as for you, ye thought evil against me; but God meant it unto good, to bring it to pass, as it is this day, to save much people alive' (*Gen.* 50:20, AV).

# 3

# In the School
# of Adversity

Though God was with Joseph in the prison and 'showed him kindness and granted him favour in the eyes of the prison warden' (Gen. 39:21), nonetheless in Pharaoh's jail Joseph was in the school of adversity. He was not only suffering for wrong he had not done, but he was there for a period of years. He had been kept in prison for some time before the cupbearer and baker 'offended their master, the king of Egypt'. How long 'some time later' (Gen. 40:1) was, we do not know. But what we do know is that when Joseph was owed a favour by the cupbearer (verse 14) that un-grateful man forgot him for 'two full years' (Gen. 41:1). Enjoying his own freedom, he failed to remember that Joseph was still deprived of his.

Joseph, then, languished for some considerable time in prison. True he had a privileged position, but that was no substitute for his lack of freedom nor for the denial of justice which he had experienced. So Joseph in prison is rightly said to be in the school of adversity, a school in which many of God's children since have been put for their spiritual profit. Such a school they do not choose for themselves. God sends them there without telling them what is in the curriculum or what lessons they will learn.

The story of Joseph, as recorded in this chapter, tells us, in effect, that God keeps us in the school of adversity just so long as He determines. If it were left to us, we would be out of it no sooner than we had entered it because we instinctively think in terms of our comfort, whereas God purposes our good (as He defines it!). Our comfort, however, seldom coincides with our good.

## 1. THE MEN GOD BROUGHT ACROSS JOSEPH'S PATH

How did the cupbearer and the baker come to be in prison? Well, for some reason or another they had 'offended their master, the king of Egypt' (verse 1). Pharaoh was so angry with them that he had them consigned to the same prison as the one in which Joseph was confined. This was not any old prison: it was 'the place where the king's prisoners were confined' (*Gen.* 39:20; see also 40:3). Just as God had placed Joseph in prison in His providence, so now he brings these two important officials across Joseph's path. He is Lord of persons as well as places.

It is not necessary that men should know God (as Joseph did) for Him to use them in the accomplishing of His will. The hearts of all are open to God, and He is able to move them to accomplish His purposes even if they do not worship and serve Him. So he moved Hiram, king of Tyre, to provide almug-wood 'to make supports for the temple of the LORD' (*1 Kings* 10:12). Likewise He moved Artaxerxes, king of Persia, to assist Nehemiah in the rebuilding of

Jerusalem (*Neh.* 2:7–8). God uses men who do not know Him to accomplish the purposes of His kingdom. He works His purposes out using most unlikely people, so that we can only marvel at His wisdom. Let us then be careful lest we misunderstand God's ways because of prejudice against the instruments He uses.

Now, had Joseph merely served the cupbearer and the baker well, he would doubtless have been forgotten and his name never mentioned to Pharaoh. Yet, though he was forgotten for a time (*Gen.* 40:23) Joseph's name was remembered (*Gen.* 41:9–13). It was remembered because he had a God-given ability to interpret dreams (*Gen.* 41:16). This ability was first demonstrated when his two distinguished charges both had a dream, each on the same night (verse 5). 'Each dream had a meaning of its own', but neither dream made sense to the two men until Joseph interpreted it, the outcome of events proving how exact his interpretation was.

The Old Testament records that on many occasions God made use of dreams to speak His Word and to make known His will. He spoke to the patriarchs in dreams – Jacob's ladder springs at once to mind (*Gen.* 28:12–15), a dream our Lord had in view when he said, 'You shall see heaven open, and the angels of God ascending and descending on the Son of Man' (*John* 1:51).

Joseph himself had had prophetic dreams, dreams whose meaning was all too clear to his brothers (*Gen.* 37:5–9). Years later, when they sought corn in Egypt, they fulfilled the dreams by bowing down before the brother they thought they would never see again. They were there as subjects of Joseph, whose king-like authority was next to that of Pharaoh.

It is clear from a careful reading of Scripture that God used dreams to communicate his mind much more frequently in the Old Testament era than in the New. This is only to be expected before the written revelation of His will that we now have in Holy Scripture was completed. While it would be going beyond the explicit teaching of the New Testament to maintain that God will never use dreams again to make himself known or to communicate a knowledge of His will, we should not be looking to dreams but to the Bible for guidance and direction.

In speaking to Joseph's two important fellow-prisoners in dreams, God shows that the hearts of men who do not know Him are nevertheless under His government. Every heart is open to Him, and He makes what impression He pleases upon them.

These two men, however, had the dreams they did because of their relationship with Joseph, the intended preserver of God's covenant people. Their dreams, and particularly that of the cupbearer, were part of the unfolding drama of God's redemption. The dreams they could not understand were to be recalled when Pharaoh had dreams that none of his magicians and wise men could interpret (Gen. 41:8).

Joseph was enabled by God to interpret Pharaoh's dreams (Gen. 41:25–36) and, in consequence, was elevated to a position of great authority. Looking back he must have marvelled at the strange twists and turns of God's providence, for his path to Pharaoh's right hand lay from the house of Potiphar through the prison to which he was unjustly consigned. God put Joseph in a place he would never have chosen to be in to further His purpose to save His people.

Sometimes we too experience the strange twists and turns of God's providence. We may, for example, be placed in a job we did not train for and which we do not like, but God has someone there to whom He wants us to speak the gospel. As He did with Joseph, He brings a person across our path for a purpose. As we have already mentioned, He is the Lord of persons as well as places.

## 2. THE BEHAVIOUR OF JOSEPH

In this chapter there are a number of indications of the godly behaviour of Joseph. It is very clear that *he depended upon God* (verse 8). Though in the form of a question, Joseph's words, 'Do not interpretations belong to God?', are in fact a declaration of his conscious dependence upon God. They are also a confession of faith in the one true God, a confession given to men who believed in many gods.

Joseph did not lean on his own understanding. Knowing the fear of the Lord, he relied upon God for wisdom (see Proverbs 1:7). So he could say in confidence to the two officials, 'Tell me your dreams.'

To the chief cupbearer, Joseph was able to declare good news. Within three days he would be released and restored to his former position (verse 13). 'When the chief baker saw that Joseph had given a favourable interpretation' (verse 16) he asked that Joseph interpret his dream. Joseph had only bad news for him – within three days he would be executed (verses 18–19) – but he did not flinch from imparting bad news. *He was as faithful in declaring bad news as he was in bringing good news.*

Joseph was not a false prophet. He did not try to soften bad news so as to make it more palatable to the chief baker. Unlike the false prophets of Jeremiah's day, he did not say

'Peace, peace', when there was no peace (*Jer.* 6:14; 8:11). Joseph was faithful to God and faithful to man.

Now supposing, dear reader, you were told that you had but three days to live. What would be your reaction? Would you be glad that you had time to seek the Lord and to prepare for eternity?

Or would you be angry with God because you do not have the time to do what you want to do? Would you put your remaining days to good use by repenting of your sins and casting yourself on Christ the Saviour of sinners? Or would you pass your last few days in revelling like the Epicureans who taught their followers to 'eat, drink, and be merry, for tomorrow we die'?

How the chief baker spent his last days we do not know. But we do know that Joseph's interpretation of his dream was right (verse 21) and that he was a faithful messenger of God. We also know that the church today needs faithful messengers who fear God more than they fear people. Too many ministers speak smooth words because, as one godly church secretary put it, they have been trained to be diplomats. So they never rebuke the sins of their people, nor warn them of the wrath to come.

Joseph shared our humanity. No one likes being in prison, particularly if they are innocent. So Joseph *sought a kindness from the chief cupbearer*. He asked that, when he was restored to favour, he would mention him to Pharaoh in order to secure his release (verse 14).

Joseph advances two reasons why the chief cupbearer should show him kindness. First, because he had been 'forcibly carried off from the land of the Hebrews' and sold into slavery (verse 15). Here Joseph appeals to the official's sense of pity.

Secondly, Joseph points out that he is innocent of the charge against him. He should not be in prison: 'Even here I have done nothing to deserve being put in a dungeon.' Here Joseph appeals to the chief cupbearer's sense of justice. He undoubtedly felt that he had a strong case, and that the official might well secure his release.

If so, *Joseph experienced disappointment* (verse 23). Enjoying his own freedom, the chief cupbearer 'did not remember Joseph; he forgot him'. What a notable instance of ingratitude!

The official should have been deeply grateful, but in his own joy at being released and restored to favour he forgot Joseph for 'two full years' (*Gen.* 41:1). He only remembered when there was a crisis at court – when no one could interpret Pharaoh's dreams (*Gen.* 40:8).

How much trust Joseph placed in the chief cupbearer we are not told. One thing is certain, and it is this – people often prove to be broken reeds. They make promises they do not keep. They turn out to be utterly unreliable. So Joseph experienced disappointment and he was quite probably cast down for a while. His hope of release had risen, only to be dashed as the days passed by into years.

Yet God was with him (*Gen.* 39: 23), the God of the covenant, the utterly faithful One who has promised never to leave nor forsake His people (*Heb.* 13:5). And God often proves His faithfulness to us against the background of the ingratitude and unfaithfulness of men.

If we use them aright, the disappointments of life will bring us closer to God. It is then that we discover the sweet consolation of resting in Him. We learn the wisdom of submitting to His will. Joseph will be released, but in God's time, not his.

### 3. Virtues Learned in the School of Adversity

There are some virtues that are most fittingly learned in the school of adversity. Indeed, they are seldom learned outside it. First, there is *submission to the will of God.*

Joseph knew why, from one point of view, he was in prison. He was there because the false accusations of an immoral woman had been believed. But why God had allowed him to be imprisoned, and what His purpose was, Joseph did not know. Yet looking back on his time in prison, Joseph could see that being in the school of adversity was all part of God's good purpose (*Gen.* 50:20).

His experience was not pleasant, but he surely learned to submit to God's will. This is one of the hardest lessons to learn in the Christian life, especially when, like Joseph, we are in a situation not of our choosing and from which we desperately long to be free.

We make submission to God's will harder if we insist on evaluating our circumstances in terms of whether or not they contribute to our happiness or our comfort. If we judge things by this consideration when we are in the school of adversity, one thing is certain: we shall rebel, rather than submit to God's will.

But if we are persuaded from Scripture, and have its truth laid upon our hearts, that God is *always* working for our good (*Rom.* 8:28), then we shall bow to God's will, for that will is holy, wise and good.

It is *holy* because, though it uses the acts of evildoers, it never compromises with sin. It is *wise*, even when we do not understand it. It is *good* when, like Joseph, we cannot see what possible good can come out of our particular circumstances. When we have such a view of the will of God, we learn to surrender ourselves to Him, and find that His will is 'good, pleasing and perfect' (*Rom.* 12:2).

There is great spiritual benefit to be had in submitting to God's will. If we really submit from the heart, we shall be freed from the anger that arises when we question, as we so easily do, God's right to put us in the school of adversity. Instead, as we submit, we find that, as Dante put it, 'In His will is our peace.'

Submission is not always instant. It is often the outcome of what may be a fierce and protracted struggle. Our Lord's agony in the Garden of Gethsemane bears witness to this (see Matthew 26:36–43).

Another virtue that is learned in the school of adversity is *patient waiting for God's deliverance*. How Joseph must have longed for his release after the chief cupbearer was given his freedom! How much he must have expected that the official would keep his promise and intercede with Pharaoh! But as the days passed – two whole years in fact – Joseph was shut up to wait for God to work. Like the psalmist he had to wait patiently for the Lord to deliver him (*Psa.* 40:1–3).

There is yet another virtue that is learned in the school of adversity. It is *resting in God alone*, without creature comforts and without the help of friends. Joseph no doubt came to rest in God alone. David certainly did. He declared,

My soul finds rest in God alone;
  My salvation comes from him.
He alone is my rock and my salvation;
  He is my fortress, I shall never be shaken.
                              (*Psa.* 62:1–2)

The school of adversity is not one that we would choose for ourselves. God sends us to it. He sent Joseph to it, and He determined when he should leave it. Joseph emerged from his time in the school of adversity both humbled and enriched. And so may we.

# 4

# From Prison
# to Palace

With Genesis chapter 41, we come to a dramatic change in Joseph's situation. He is released from prison, not to return as a slave to Potiphar's household, but to be put in a position of great power and influence. Joseph is elevated to the highest place in the land, with only Pharaoh above him in importance. Thus did Pharaoh decree: 'You shall be in charge of my palace, and all my people are to submit to your orders. Only with respect to the throne will I be greater than you' (*Gen.* 41:40).

## 1. OUT OF PRISON

Joseph's dramatic change of circumstances – from prison to palace – came about because Pharaoh had two vivid prophetic dreams in the same night. In both, a time of plenty was succeeded by a time of poverty. First, seven cows, 'sleek and fat' were devoured by seven 'ugly and gaunt' cows (verses 2–3). Then, in a second dream, 'seven heads of corn, healthy and good' and growing on a single stalk (verse 5) were 'swallowed up' by seven thin heads of corn that had been scorched by the east wind (verses 6–7). These two dreams deeply troubled Pharaoh, so much so that, in the morning, 'he sent for all the magicians and wise men of Egypt' (verse 8). He told them his dreams, but none of these professionals was able to interpret them.

Suddenly the chief cupbearer remembered the man whom he had forgotten, Joseph the servant of the captain of the guard (verse 12). He told Pharaoh of the accuracy of Joseph's interpretation of dreams: 'Things turned out exactly as he interpreted them to us: I was restored to my position, and the other man was hanged' (verse 13). Hearing this Pharaoh immediately sent for Joseph who, having been given a quick wash and brush up (verse 14), was brought before the king.

As before Pharaoh's servants in prison, so now before Pharaoh himself, Joseph pointed to God's wisdom, not his own. 'God', he said, 'will give Pharaoh the answer he desires' (verse 16).

The two dreams have the same basic meaning. Seven years of plenty would be followed by seven years of famine. Their sombre message is underlined by God. The reason why the dream was given in two forms was that 'the matter has been firmly decided by God' (verse 32). Pharaoh must take urgent action to make provision for the years of famine for 'God will do it soon'.

Joseph not only interpreted Pharaoh's dreams; he also gave him wise counsel (verses 33–36). He proposed that commissioners be appointed for every district. These would set aside a fifth of the harvest during the seven years of plenty. This would be stored in the cities and kept in reserve, to be made available to feed the population in the years of famine. A supremo should be appointed to oversee the work of the commissioners, 'a discerning and wise man' who would report directly to Pharaoh. The king was so impressed by the wisdom of Joseph that he appointed him as his chief executive officer (verse 40).

In all these events we see the marvellous workings of God's providence. Joseph exchanges Pharaoh's prison for Pharaoh's palace so that when there is famine in Canaan there will be corn in Egypt to keep his family alive (Gen. 50:20). The God who made the covenant promises will see to it that the covenant family will not perish from hunger.

There is much that we can learn from this chapter of the workings of God's providence in the life of Joseph. The first lesson is that Joseph was not released from prison until it was time to interpret Pharaoh's dreams.

### i. Not Before Time

At least two years before his release (verse 1) Joseph had seen what appeared to be an opportunity to get out of prison very soon (Gen. 40:14–15). The chief cupbearer owed him a favour, so, 'Surely', Joseph thought, 'he will put in a good word for me with the king when the opportunity arises.' Being human, Joseph naturally wanted his freedom, and now it looked as if he would soon obtain it. But the chief cupbearer 'did not remember Joseph; he forgot him' (Gen. 40:23).

Joseph's hope of a quick release was dashed. He stayed in prison for at least two more years, no doubt bitterly disappointed for a time.

Now let us suppose that Joseph had been soon released from prison through the good offices of the chief cupbearer. It would have been highly unlikely that he would have been given a position of great authority that he could eventually use to save the lives of his family. Perhaps, out of gratitude, the chief cupbearer might have bought Joseph's freedom, and he would have returned to his own land. If so, he would not have been at hand to interpret Pharaoh's dreams and, in consequence, he would not have been raised to his exalted position.

When Joseph was in a position to do his family good, he could look back and appreciate God's wisdom in not permitting his release two full years earlier. Then – and only then – was he able to see that God meant it for good.

What happened to Joseph is very instructive. Like him, we too can be disappointed by God's delays. What appears to us to be an opportunity to get out of an unpleasant situation does not come to pass. We may, for example, have to stay in an uncongenial job when we had high hopes of obtaining a better position in another firm. What seems to us a good way out does not open up because God wants to bring us into a place of usefulness much larger than we could ever have imagined. God sometimes disappoints our hopes, not to cause us needless grief, but to fulfil a purpose in our lives that, at the time, we could not have envisaged. Joseph could not see beyond the prison walls, but God could see to Pharaoh's palace – and far beyond! Unless you and I realize that our God sees far beyond our limited horizons we shall become disappointed and dispirited. Again we must learn to 'trust where we cannot trace'.

There is another point to be noted, and it is this. During the two years or more that Joseph remained in prison he did not know the reason for the delay. God did not see fit to tell him.

## ii. No Reason Given

God did not break his silence. Joseph remained in ignorance. It was only when Pharaoh had his two dreams that Joseph alone could interpret that Joseph could begin to understand God's purpose. Meanwhile he had to walk by faith – to look to the unseen God who works all things after the counsel of his own will. He had to remain confined in prison without knowing the real reason why he was there.

He could have spent his time bemoaning his fate. He might have fretted; but we are not told that he did. He could even have raged against God, but the narrative gives no indication that he did. Joseph could have brooded on the injustice that had landed him in prison. He could have blamed God for His apparent indifference, and even lost all faith in Him. But, had he done so, he would have acted in ignorance of the real reason why God kept him in prison – to save many people alive.

In our foolish ignorance, it is very easy to murmur against God when times are hard. The Israelites 'grumbled in their tents' (*Deut.* 1:27) when the difficulty of conquering Canaan became apparent to them. We must not imitate them. We must follow William Cowper's counsel:

> *Judge not the Lord by feeble sense*
> *But trust Him for His grace;*
> *Behind a frowning providence*
> *He hides a smiling face.*

We could only rightly judge God if we were in possession of all the facts, if we knew – as we do not! – every aspect of His purpose. But we are not in possession of all the facts. So in our prison house – in our season in the school of adversity –

we are not to judge God. Instead we are to wait patiently for Him.

We must notice a third point. The reason for Joseph's being left in prison only became apparent in the light of later events.

### iii. The Light of Later Events

The interpretation that God gave Joseph of Pharaoh's two dreams made it clear that there would be a seven-year famine in Egypt, after seven years of abundant harvests. The two dreams, of course, centre upon the Nile (verses 1, 3 and 17), whose yearly flood was vital to the fertility of the land. Nothing was said, however, about famine occurring in Canaan and other lands because of a failure in the seasonal rains. But it was famine in Canaan that was to drive Joseph's brothers to seek corn in Egypt (verse 57; *Gen.* 42:1–2).

It was only after his brothers had been driven to Egypt in search of food and stood before him that Joseph knew the real reason why he had been sold into slavery and thrown into prison. Only then could Joseph make his two memorable confessions: 'God sent me ahead of you . . . God intended it for good' (*Gen.* 45:5; 50:20). God's purpose in keeping him in prison until it was time to interpret Pharaoh's dream could only be understood at a much later stage. It was only with the advantage of hindsight that Joseph could grasp that purpose.

Indeed, providence is always to be interpreted backwards. It must never be read as if it were prophecy – events predicted in advance. For we do not, and cannot, know what the next chapter in its unfolding story will be. Providence has so many surprising twists and turns to it that it is rightly described as mysterious. It is a standing reminder to us that God's ways are not our ways.

God, unlike us, does not need the advantage of hindsight. He sees the end from the beginning. We do not, for we are finite, not infinite. We are creatures, not God. Our knowledge is limited, whereas He is omniscient, knowing past, present and future in the same moment. So we have to wait for God to make his purpose plain through the unfolding of events. We have to remember that

> *God is his own interpreter*
> *And he will make it plain.*

We must refuse to jump to a hasty conclusion when God's providence brings us into dark days. Either here, or hereafter, he will make His purpose plain. Meanwhile, we must be prepared to live in mystery.

## 2. Prepared for the Palace

After Joseph had interpreted Pharaoh's dreams and given him wise counsel (verses 33–36), it was obvious to Pharaoh that Joseph was the man to be put in charge of affairs (verses 38–39). Though a foreigner, Joseph was put in a position of great influence, next in importance only to Pharaoh (verse 40). Pharaoh gave him his signet ring (verse 42), which meant that he could sign documents with the equivalent of royal authority. Joseph was also given clothes suitable to his office and a chariot in which to ride (verse 43) – an ancient counterpart to a ministerial Daimler! An Egyptian name – Zaphenath-Paneah – and an Egyptian wife – Asenath – were also given to him.

What a dramatic change in Joseph's circumstances! In one day he went from a prison to a palace, from being a prisoner to being Prime Minister, from the status of a powerless slave to that of an extremely powerful official!

Such a change in his position could well have proved too much for Joseph to handle. His new power could easily have gone to his head. Prosperity proves the undoing of many; but it was not so in the case of Joseph, for he had been thoroughly prepared for it whilst in the school of adversity.

### i. A Long Preparation

First of all, in this school he had a long preparation. If we compare Genesis 37:2 with 41:46, we find that Joseph was a slave and a prisoner in Egypt *for thirteen years* before he was elevated to his position of power and influence. Why so long? Surely it was because God was preparing Joseph for his office. The character required for such an office is not produced overnight but over years – especially in a young, priggish man like Joseph.

Today we live in the age of the 'instant'. We forget that God does not. His ways are often much slower than ours, because He puts a much greater value on tried character than we do! He is not impressed by 'whizz kids' who are sometimes given places of leadership within our churches with disastrous consequences.

The essential thing for a would-be Christian leader is to be a ready learner in the school of adversity – to submit to God's process of fashioning His servant for the work He has in view for him. How long God keeps anyone in this school is His business – not ours!

### ii. A Thorough Preparation

Secondly, in the school of adversity Joseph received a thorough preparation for high office. When he was an unwise, bumptious young man he needlessly provoked resentment in his brothers by telling his dreams to them. But, as a slave and a prisoner, God was preparing him for future service.

He was taught *humility*. Joseph was the pampered, favourite son of Jacob. No doubt others served him. As a slave and a prisoner, he had to serve others. What a comedown for Joseph! But he had to accept it. He had to learn to serve others with humility so that, when he was given great power to exercise, he would not abuse it.

A humble man is able to handle power without being corrupted by it. We see this supremely in our Lord Jesus Christ who, though the world was made through Him, humbled Himself and became a servant (*Phil.* 2:7). Only a man humbled, like Joseph, in the school of adversity could have coped with his sudden transition to the exercise of great power. When he was in a position to do his brothers great harm, he humbly confessed that God had used their cruel action for good!

Joseph learned something else in the school of adversity – his own *inability*. If he fancied himself when a youth in his father's house, his long years of preparation changed his outlook. More than once he confesses his own inability (*Gen.* 40:8; 45:16). 'I cannot do it' (*Gen.* 41:16) are not words that Joseph would have uttered when a youth; but now he is happy to acknowledge his inability.

Distrust in one's own ability is the precondition for receiving divine wisdom (*James* 1:5). To foreswear trust in our own ability – and to look habitually to God's ability – is not a lesson easily learned. Perhaps this is one reason why Joseph was so long in the school of adversity.

Finally, Joseph was taught *the management of affairs*. First in Potiphar's household (*Gen.* 39:4–6), and then in prison (*Gen.* 39:21–23), Joseph was given a position of responsibility. In both places he was being trained in the methods of Egyptian administration for the day when God would give the management of the whole of Egypt into his hands. God was seeing to it that Joseph did not come to the administration of Egypt's affairs as a novice. The counsel that Joseph gave to Pharaoh demonstrates that he had learned much in the years of preparation. It was because of this that he was able to rise to the challenge of storing huge quantities of corn in the years of plenty, ready for the years of dearth (verses 48–49).

Joseph's years in the school of adversity were years of preparation for the power he would exercise in the palace of Pharaoh. They were hard but profitable years. They were not wasted by Joseph becoming bitter in soul. They were years in which he became a useful, humble servant of God.

What of *our* seasons of trial and adversity? Do we use them aright, realizing that they are never unrelated to the service that God has in store for us? Our times of adversity are never to be isolated in our thinking from the total pattern of our lives. They are not times when God has abandoned us, but times of preparation for the fulfilling of His greater purposes for us.

> *Leave to His sovereign sway*
> *To choose and to command;*
> *So shalt thou, wondering, own His way,*
> *How wise, how strong, His hand.*

> *Far, far above thy thought*
> *His counsel shall appear,*
> *When fully He the work hath wrought*
> *That caused thy needless fear.*

*Thou seest our weakness, Lord;*
*Our hearts are known to Thee.*
*O lift Thou up the sinking hand,*
*Confirm the feeble knee.*

Paul Gerhardt
(translated by John Wesley)

# 5

# Physician
# of Souls

With chapter 42 of Genesis, we enter upon a new stage in the life of Joseph. In the countries surrounding Egypt a severe famine prevails. But in Egypt itself there is food, because of Joseph's wisdom in ordering that the good harvests of the years of plenty should be stored up to meet the needs of the years of dearth.

There is great want in the household of Jacob, but he learns that there is corn in Egypt (*Gen.* 42:1). So the patriarch sends ten of his sons down into Egypt to buy corn for the whole family. Unbeknown to them their long lost brother Joseph now stands next to Pharaoh in honour and importance. He is 'the governor of the land, the one who sold corn to all its people' (verse 6).

When the ten brothers arrive, they bow down before their long-lost brother. They do not recognize him, which is not surprising, for they did not know whether he was dead or alive. They come as suppliants to one who has their life in his hands, for, should he refuse to supply them with corn, they and their families will starve.

What irony there is in the spectacle of the ten brothers prostrating themselves before their long-lost brother! Years before Joseph unwisely told them about a strange dream that he had.

In this dream their sheaves bowed down to Joseph's sheaf (*Gen.* 37:7). His brothers' reaction was predictable. 'Do you intend to reign over us? Will you actually rule us?' they exclaimed (verse 8). They were so consumed by the hatred that this dream provoked in them that, when the opportunity came, they sold Joseph into slavery without pity (verse 28). Returning home with his blood-stained coat, they succeeded in persuading their father Jacob that his favourite son was dead.

Now in this ironic scene they prostrate themselves before the brother whom they do not recognize. Twenty or so years have passed and they come in their time of need to Egypt to seek a favour from Pharaoh's governor, who is in fact their brother.

Why did not Joseph tell his brothers who he was the moment he recognized them? How glad their father would have been to hear that the son he had given up for dead was still alive! At first sight Joseph's behaviour is hard to understand. It is enigmatic, strange. Yet, if we remember that God gave Joseph great wisdom (*Gen.* 41:39), we shall pause before criticizing him for concealing his identity and acting in the way he did.

It seems to me that in chapters 42–44, Joseph appears as a wise and compassionate *physician of souls*. Before this point in the story, he is brought before us as a man of God-given wisdom who is able to interpret dreams that no one else is able to understand.

Joseph is also portrayed as a man of great administrative ability who can take charge of Potiphar's affairs and the prisoners in the jail in which he was put. But now as the story unfolds further Joseph appears in a new light. Let us then consider Joseph as a physician of souls, and see what we can learn of spiritual profit for ourselves.

## 1. KINDNESS IN DISGUISE

First, though he speaks harshly to his brothers Joseph does not act vindictively towards them. 'He pretended to be a stranger and spoke harshly to them' (verse 7). Perhaps this was to hide his true feelings, but more probably he wants to steer them to the point of recognizing their own lack of pity in selling him into slavery (verse 21).

Later when the brothers returned to Canaan and reported to Jacob what had happened to them they remembered the harsh treatment they had received. 'The man who is lord over the land spoke harshly to us and treated us as though we were spying on the land' (verse 30).

Yet throughout Joseph is not acting vindictively towards his brothers, for he has to turn away from them in order to give expression to his true feelings (verse 24; see also Gen. 43:30; 45:1–2). Such tender weeping does not go with a vindictive, vengeful spirit.

Joseph was not in any way motivated by a desire to get even with his brothers. His seeming harshness sprang from a different source altogether.

Let us learn from Joseph not to harbour a vindictive spirit, especially when we are wronged by those nearest and dearest to us. Joseph is a good example to us of not paying back evil with evil (*Rom.* 12:17). He teaches us how to treat those who wrong us (*Rom.* 12:20). He points us to the Lord Jesus Christ, of whom in this respect he is a type (*1 Pet.* 2:23).

## 2. LOVE CONCEALED

Secondly, Joseph's harshness conceals a loving attitude towards his brothers. Certainly, he conceals his identity when he might have revealed it (verse 7). Certainly, he speaks harshly to them and accuses them of being spies when he knew that they were not. Of course, to his brothers Joseph must have appeared as a man to be feared and not loved. Yet all the time Joseph has the deepest, tenderest feelings towards them. However, he does not allow his feelings to rule his behaviour because first he has to bring them to repentance. It is only when they have had a taste of prison themselves that they begin to acknowledge their sin (verse 21).

If Joseph had immediately revealed his true identity to his brothers the moment he recognized them, it is doubtful whether his brothers would have appreciated the enormity of what they had done so long before. They first had to be ploughed and harrowed before they brought forth the fruit of repentance. To the brothers, Pharaoh's governor seemed exceedingly harsh, a man from whom no mercy could be expected. Yet, all the time, Joseph's harshness conceals a loving attitude towards them.

There is a very real sense in which Joseph's harsh and strange behaviour reflects the way in which God himself deals with sinners towards whom from eternity He has a loving purpose of grace. He thunders against our sins in His law. Through His law we behold Him as the God of Sinai, so awesome in His power and holiness that we are filled with fear. Then it seems that there is no mercy to be found in Him. He is all wrath, as Luther imagined while he trembled under conviction of sin. Many since Luther have thought exactly the same. God seems only to have a harsh face – severe and condemning. There is no smile on it.

Why does God treat sinners so harshly? Because He would have us learn the sinfulness of sin. He wants us to know our guilt and to recognize our wickedness. He furrows our consciences with His law. He employs His law to make our sin 'become utterly sinful' (*Rom.* 7:13) to us. God must do His 'strange work' (*Isa.* 28:21), yet all the time he loves the sinners for whom His Son died. The death of Christ proves this beyond a shadow of a doubt: 'God demonstrates his own love for us in this: While we were still sinners, Christ died for us' (*Rom.* 5:8).

## 3. REPENTANCE SOUGHT

Thirdly, Joseph's treatment of his brothers is designed to bring them to repentance. More than one possible course of action was open to Joseph when his brothers stood before him, not recognizing who he was (verse 8).

He could have sent them away empty-handed, without pity. They, after all, had shown no pity to him when they had sold him into slavery so many years before (verse 21). But he was not vindictive. Joseph could not send them away without the provisions for which they had come to Egypt.

Joseph could also have supplied his brothers' wants and concealed his identity from them forever. Had he taken this course of action it would have been understandable, since they had cast him out of their family. If they did not want him in their family, why should Joseph want to be part of them again? But far from wanting to keep his distance from his brothers Joseph desired to be reunited with them (*Gen.* 45:15).

Joseph could have taken yet another course of action. He could have supplied his brothers' needs and then revealed his true identity to them immediately. However, he did not know whether they still hated him. Nor could he know then whether his brothers were truly sorry for their sin. So Joseph took the only wise course of action, as a physician of souls. He acted towards his brothers in a way that was designed to bring them to repentance.

First, *he made them realize that they were in a position of great danger.* He accused them of being spies who had come into Egypt in order 'to see where our land is unprotected' (verses 9, 12 and 14).

Egypt was open to invasion from Canaan. Its northern frontier was its most vulnerable. So the Egyptians were always very suspicious of Canaanite travellers. Joseph knew this – and so did his brothers. Therefore when he accused them of being spies they must have trembled. They knew that they were in the governor of Egypt's power – power that he exercised when he consigned them to prison for three days (verse 17). Without a doubt, their lives were in his hands.

Joseph's accusation was, of course, a contrived one. But God's accusations against us are never that. They are always completely true, always completely just. They are designed to arouse us to a sense of danger. If we are wise we will 'be afraid of the One (God himself) who can destroy both soul and body in hell' (*Matt.* 10:28).

[47]

It is not pleasant, but it is good, when God alarms and awakens us to our danger. When this happens we become aware that God has not left us in our sins. He has, despite the thundering of His law, a gracious purpose toward us. So it was with Joseph's seemingly harsh behaviour towards his brothers. He alarmed them, not to leave them always in a state of terror, but to open their hearts to his later expressions of mercy.

Secondly, *Joseph gave his brothers a taste of prison* (verses 15–17). Once his brothers in their blind hatred of Joseph had consigned him to prison in an empty cistern (*Gen.* 37:24). There Joseph was left without food and water. Now their brief taste of prison life led his brothers to begin to recognize their own guilt. 'Surely we are being punished because of our own brother. We saw how distressed he was when he pleaded with us for his life, but we would not listen' (verse 21).

Years before, Joseph's brothers had acted without pity. They had closed their ears to Joseph's cries for mercy, but now they could see that God's righteous hand was against them, 'therefore is this distress come upon us'. The severe treatment that they now received was necessary to awaken their consciences for, despite the pleas of Reuben (verse 22; compare *Gen.* 37:21–22, 29–30), they had gone ahead with their plan to get rid of Joseph.

For many years – at least twenty, probably twenty-two – their consciences appear to have slumbered. They kept up their deception of their father Jacob (*Gen.* 37:31–33). They did not go down to Egypt to look for their brother. They only went to Egypt when necessity, not conscience, drove them there. It was only when they had a taste of prison that they began to feel what they should have felt long ago – their guilt before God.

Again Joseph mirrors the ways of God with us. Sometimes He must act severely against us because only thus can He arouse our consciences from their slumber. He must make our way hard and our lot unpleasant, because, in prosperity and ease, we have no thought of His holiness and of our sin. So God must deal with us severely. He assails us until our stubborn wills bend and we admit our guilt before God.

God may send our hopes crashing to the ground. He takes our possessions from us, our job, or a loved one through death – so that we start to see our folly and our guilt in living without Him for so long. It was so with the prodigal son (*Luke* 15:11–24). He had to come to the pig trough (verses 15–16) before he came to his senses (verse 17) and began his journey back home.

From the unfavourable demeanour of the governor, and the harsh treatment they had received, Joseph's brothers could have argued that he was implacably opposed to them. If they did draw this conclusion they would have been quite wrong (verse 24). The strokes he laid upon them were not given out of hatred but out of love. They were deserved but their not-yet-known brother took no delight in their plight – far from it. His severity was but the other side of his goodness. His great desire was to bring them to repentance.

Again Joseph in a real sense mirrors the ways of God with us sinners (*Rom.* 11:22). When experiencing God's goodness does not issue in repentance God will visit stubborn sinners with His severity. His severity is but the other side of His goodness, for when His severity leads to repentance His merciful purpose is likewise accomplished. It is good when a person is able to say, 'This severity – this affliction – this sorrow – is not a fraction of what I deserve for my sins. Then why should I complain? Why should I not turn from my sins to God and bless Him for every stroke of His that has brought me to my senses?'

Joseph did not leave his brothers in prison. Though for a time he treated them severely, he did not leave them without hope. They spent only three days in prison (*Gen.* 42:17) whereas Joseph had probably spent three years there. George Lawson aptly observes: 'If Joseph's goodness had not been regulated by wisdom, he would not have committed his brethren to prison. If his wisdom had not been sweetened with goodness and compassion, he might have left them in prison till their spirits failed, or were exasperated by harsh treatment, and till their poor father and his family were ready to perish with want.'[1]

Thirdly, *Joseph gave his brothers indications of his grace towards them*, though these served only to alarm them further (verses 25–28, 35). Joseph ordered that the silver with which his brothers had paid for the corn should be hidden in their bags. He also gave them provisions for their journey back home.

When they stopped for the night, one of them opened his sack to get food for his donkey. He discovered that his silver had been returned to him (verse 28). This discovery filled them with alarm. They were even more alarmed when, on their arrival home, each of them discovered that his silver had been given back. Not only were they afraid, but so was their father Jacob (verse 35).

Joseph's grace towards his brothers (and grace it was, for they received that for which they were not, in the end,

[1] George Lawson: *The Life of Joseph*, 1807; reprinted Edinburgh: Banner of Truth, 1972, pp. 142–3).

required to pay) alarmed them. For they were not yet reconciled to him, or he to them (see *Gen.* 45:3, 15). The money in their sacks looked to them like a trick, which it was not (verse 28).

Joseph's behaviour was an enigma to them. They mistook his grace for severity, the seeking of a further ground to accuse them of being thieves as well as spies. Again we can learn something of God's ways in all this. When God ploughs deep into your conscience and you begin to see the sinfulness of sin, you find it hard to believe that God can show you any grace.

Yet, like Joseph, He gives you tokens of His grace, to encourage you. He may impress a promise of His Word upon your mind, or speak to you through a sermon, in order to encourage you to exercise faith in Christ. Be sure that you value such tokens of grace, and use them so that you come to a full repentance and deep faith in Jesus Christ, the only Saviour of sinners.

The Puritans often employed what they termed 'Uses' to drive home their preaching of God's Word. I shall do the same at the end of this chapter.

USE 1. *If you have a faithful physician of souls as your pastor be thankful.* You may not have appreciated his straightness at first. Now you may be coming to see that as a good physician of souls he is bringing home to you the seriousness of your sin. Be thankful to God, for today there are too many ministers who merit God's charge that they heal the hurt of His people superficially. They cry 'Peace, peace' in God's Name, when there is no peace (*Jer.* 6:14), for their hearers still slumber in their sins.

You would not thank a surgeon for giving you a flesh wound when your disease required that he cut deep in order to bring about your healing. So thank God for faithful pastors, true physicians of souls, whose cuts go deep and whose medicine is severe, but whom God uses to heal precious souls.

Pray for such pastors, that they may be kept faithful, not bowing to the insidious pressure to tone down the message of the gospel. Pastors today, as in the past, are always exposed to the danger of doing a shallow work in order to win favour with some church members. They need our prayers very much indeed.

USE 2. *Pray that wisdom and insight be given to those to whom God has committed the care of souls.* What great need they have! Compassion without wisdom can be foolish. Wisdom without compassion can be cold and heartless. So pray much for your pastor and God will grant you a great return for your prayers.

USE 3. *Respond as you ought to the wounds that you must have if you are to be cured of sin.* Do not rebel when the Word of God cuts deep. Do not complain when your conscience is aroused. Do not look for superficial healing, for shallow comfort. Pray with Augustus Toplady:

> Be of sin the double cure,
> Cleanse me from its guilt and power.

The strokes of God the Father, in His providence and through the preaching of His Word, are designed to drive you to the wounds of the crucified Saviour. Go then to the cross of Calvary, and you will find that there your wounds will be healed. For the cross is the

> *Sweet resting place of every heart*
>    *That feels the plague of sin,*
> *Yet knows that deep mysterious joy,*
>    *The peace of God within.*

Edward Denny

# 6

# Testing and Comforting

When Joseph's brothers went back to Canaan they had to leave Simeon behind as a pledge of their honesty (Gen. 42:37) and as surety that they would return with their youngest brother Benjamin (verse 34).

Jacob their father put the worst possible gloss on Simeon's failure to return. So far as he was concerned his son had suffered the same fate as his long lost son Joseph: 'Joseph is no more and Simeon is no more' (verse 36). Both sons were dead. Now, added to that tragedy, he is faced with the demand that his youngest son Benjamin be taken down to Egypt. No wonder Jacob exclaimed, 'Everything is against me!'

Chapter 43 opens with the recounting of the overcoming of Jacob's reluctance to let Benjamin go. Judah points out that the brothers cannot return to Egypt to buy more food unless they take Benjamin with them. He emphasizes how adamant the governor of Egypt was when they stood before him: 'The man warned us solemnly, "You will not see my face again unless your brother is with you"' (*Gen*. 43:3,5).

Jacob reproaches the brothers for disclosing to the Egyptian overlord the fact that they had a brother at home. In their defence, Judah points out that they could not help giving this information (verse 7). He then pledges himself to take full responsibility for Benjamin's safety (verse 9).

Reluctantly, Jacob agrees to let Benjamin go with his brothers on their next journey to Egypt (verse 11). So they set off bearing a courtesy gift (verse 11) and double the amount of silver needed in order to cover what they had found in their sacks. As they depart Jacob commits them to the care of God Almighty – El-Shaddai – the name of God that is peculiarly associated with the patriarchal period (See *Gen*. 17:1; 28:3; 35:11; 48:3).

When the brothers present themselves to Joseph (verse 15), he still acts towards them as a physician of souls. Yet his behaviour is somewhat different from what it was on their first visit, for now they have proved that what they had said was true – Benjamin was with them (verse 16). So now Joseph offers them the hospitality of his house.

## 1. TESTING

The brothers' testing is described in Genesis 43:26–34 and 44:1–17. The treatment they receive on this their second visit is in stark contrast to what they had experienced on their first visit. This time they are not cast into prison, but are received as honoured guests in Joseph's house. Their invitation to a noon meal, however, frightens them. They thought that their number was up: 'We were brought here because of the silver that was put back into our sacks the first time. He wants to attack us and overpower us and seize us as slaves and take our donkeys' (verse 18).

The brothers explain to Joseph's steward how they had found the exact amount of silver that they had paid for food hidden in their sacks. This amount they now want to return. They confess their complete ignorance as to how the silver came to be in their sacks in the first place (verses 19–22). The steward tells them not to worry, for the corn has been paid for. In a statement of enigmatic ambiguity, which may perhaps hint that he knew their real identity, he testifies to the gracious provision of God: 'Your God, and the God of your father, has given you treasure in your sacks' (verse 23).

When Joseph returns home he receives his brothers' gifts and their obeisance (verse 26). He then enquires of their father – and his! But when he sees Benjamin, his own natural brother, he cannot control his emotions any longer. He hurries out in order to weep in private (verse 30). Having washed his face and regained his composure he orders the food to be served (verse 31).

Then comes the first test. Joseph has Benjamin served with five times as much food as his brothers (verse 34). Yet Benjamin is the youngest, and he is seated the furthest from him. Why does Joseph single out Benjamin in this way? The answer is clear. By his favouring of Benjamin, Joseph designs to test his brothers. Will they show toward Benjamin, who is now their father's favourite son, the same kind of envy which led them to sell Joseph into slavery (see *Gen.* 37:3–4)? Will their envy lead to hatred towards the favoured one, as it did towards Joseph years before?

This time there is no such reaction from Joseph's brothers. They accepted the favoured position of Benjamin without demur. So they passed the first test that Joseph set them.

However, it seems that Joseph may have thought that his brothers could be concealing their true feelings behind a mask of politeness. After all they are his guests and they would not question his right as their host to apportion the helpings of food as he wished. So Joseph sets his brothers a second, much more severe, test. This time he will test their willingness to suffer on behalf of Benjamin. He instructs his steward to give his brothers as much food as they can carry (*Gen.* 44:1). The silver with which they had paid for it is to be put into the mouth of their sacks, and his divining cup (verses 2 and 5) is to be hidden in Benjamin's sack.

When the next morning dawns the brothers are sent on their way but, before they get far from the city, they are pursued, halted and accused of theft (verses 4–6). They protest their innocence and argue that their past behaviour in returning the silver (verse 8) demonstrates that they are not thieves. They declare that if any one of them is found guilty he will die (verse 9), and the rest of them will become slaves.

The steward assures them that this will not be necessary – only the one who has the cup will die (verse 9). When the bags are searched – one by one, beginning with the eldest – the cup is found in Benjamin's sack. The brothers then tear their clothes in a united display of family solidarity, which stands in sharp contrast to their treatment of Joseph many years before.

Returning to the city the brothers are confronted by Joseph and they prostrate themselves before him (verse 14). Their acknowledgement of guilt has a double meaning (verse 16). Judah, who acts as their spokesman, points out that though they are not guilty of theft, they cannot prove their innocence. The cup has been found in Benjamin's sack, after all. In this sense, 'God has uncovered' their guilt. The hidden cup has been revealed and it accuses them before the overlord.

Yet, in a much deeper sense, God has uncovered their guilt with respect to Joseph. He, through Joseph, is working against the brothers in judgment until they acknowledge their sin in selling their brother into slavery in Egypt. Joseph's brothers accept their lot: 'We are now my lord's slaves', they declare (verse 16). Then Joseph puts before them a way of escape. Each of them may have his freedom at the price of the enslaving of Benjamin (verse 17).

At this point Judah approaches Joseph. In a most moving plea he offers his own life as a substitute for Benjamin's. He will take his place as a slave (verse 33). Judah's plea centres on what the failure of Benjamin to return home would do to his father, Jacob. His father is aged and Benjamin is the son of his old age (verse 20).

Benjamin is the 'only one of his mother's sons left' for his natural brother has, his father believes, been 'torn to pieces' (verse 28). 'To lose this son will break our father's heart, for his life is closely bound up with the boy's life' (verse 30). If they do not return Benjamin to their father, they will, declares Judah, 'bring the grey head of our father down to the grave in sorrow' (verse 31). Since he has guaranteed Benjamin's safety (verse 32), he pleads to be allowed to take his place as Joseph's slave (verse 33), if Joseph will let the boy go free.

In his willingness to sacrifice his own life to secure Benjamin's freedom, Judah shows how deep is the work of God in his soul, and we may assume this is also the case with his brothers. When they sold Joseph into slavery years before, all they wanted was to get him out of their lives once and for all. Then they had shown no concern for their father Jacob, and for years they had deceived him into thinking that Joseph was dead. But now they would do anything to save their father's favourite son and to spare him the misery that his loss would entail (verse 34).

At this point in the story Joseph breaks down. He can no longer control himself (*Gen.* 45:1). He dismisses his attendants and then gives way to a burst of sobbing so intense that it could be heard outside the room (verse 2). He reveals his identity to his brothers who, not surprisingly, are 'terrified at his presence' (verse 3).

Why did Joseph break down at this point? Surely it is because Judah's moving plea shows that brotherly affection for Benjamin was now strong enough to conquer self-interest. As before, so now, there was still a favourite son in the family – Benjamin, the youngest son. But, instead of hating him, the brothers are prepared to sacrifice for him. Judah is willing to take his place as a slave.

Joseph had set this severe test in order to prove the genuineness of their repentance. And now he has abundant evidence that the brothers had changed, that their old attitudes of resentment and hatred towards a favoured son had gone.

There are two important lessons to be learned from the story of Joseph's dealings with his brethren up to this point.

The first is that *a work of true repentance often takes considerable time*. It took at least two visits to Egypt, harsh words (*Gen.* 42:7) and a taste of prison (verses 15–17). It also took accusations that sounded like the padding steps of the hound of hell. It took severe tests – tests that were at once opportunities to show repentance and challenges to repent.

Why did the work of repentance take so long a time? Why was the process so drawn out? It was because their consciences had slumbered for years. The brothers had neither confessed their deceit to their father Jacob nor come down to Egypt to find Joseph. Their consciences were calloused and severely hardened. They had to be awakened, and the enormity of their sin had to come to the forefront of their moral consciousness.

This took time, for the hardened conscience is seldom made tender overnight. Joseph as a faithful physician of souls knew this, so he took time. He used means to alarm them and to bring them to a living fear of God (See *Gen.* 42:28; 44:16). He wanted the work of repentance to be deep and genuine. So he was not prepared to hurry them into a confession of their sins that would have been superficial and probably only temporary.

Joseph could not be charged with the fault of the false prophets and priests of Jeremiah's day. 'From the least to the greatest, all are greedy for gain; prophets and priests alike, all practise deceit. They dress the wound of my people as though it were not serious. "Peace, peace," they say, when there is no peace' (*Jer.* 6:13–14).

Those who heal wounds superficially are no friends to sinners, for they leave them secure in their sins, unaware of sin's enormity in God's sight. Joseph, however, was a true friend to his brothers. He had their deepest interests at heart even though his harsh and sometimes enigmatic behaviour seemed strange to them.

As remarked earlier, we live today in the age of the *instant*. We want a quick fix, whether from antibiotics for our ailments or from counselling for our personal problems. I fear that the 'instant' mentality has invaded the church. We want instant 'conversions', without deep repentance. We want additions to our church rolls without waiting for God to do His work in the soul. We want quantity above quality.

Let us learn from Joseph's dealings with his brothers that the work of repentance takes time. Let us pray much and persevere much that the fruits of repentance appear in many lives.

The second lesson to be learned from Joseph's story is that *it requires discernment to know when the work of repentance has been thoroughly done.* Joseph did not disclose his true identity to his brothers, nor seek to reassure them that they were forgiven, until he was sure that the work of repentance had been thoroughly effected. He did not reveal himself after the first test when he so blatantly favoured Benjamin. He waited until there was firm proof in Judah's passionate pleading for Benjamin that the severity that he had shown the brothers on their first visit had brought forth the fruit of repentance. In all his dealings with his brothers Joseph appears as a man of spiritual wisdom, a true pastor.

Wise, discerning pastors are one of God's greatest gifts to his church. Pray for many to be raised up – true, wise, godly physicians of souls. Pray, too, that they may be given daily wisdom – wisdom not to shrink from using drastic surgery where necessary, and wisdom not to prolong it a moment longer than is needful. Pastors need wisdom to know how deep and how long to wound, and when the time has come to comfort awakened souls.

## 2. COMFORTING

The comforting of Joseph's brothers is described in Genesis 45:1–15. When Joseph reveals who he is to his brothers they are thoroughly alarmed. Laden down with guilt as they already are, they expect no mercy, only revenge. No doubt to their surprise, Joseph now beautifully comforts them by directing them to the previously hidden, now revealed, purpose of God. 'And now', he says, 'do not be distressed and do not be angry with yourselves for selling me here, because it was to save lives that God sent me ahead of you' (verse 5).

Joseph's previous severity towards his brothers had all along concealed his compassionate heart. Now severity gives place to a ministry of comfort. Now Joseph pours into their wounds a comforting balm.

What can we learn from this? First, *if Joseph had not comforted his brothers at this point, he would have driven them to utter despair.* Their consciences had been sorely wounded. Their sense of guilt was profound, and rightly so. Yet to have a profound sense of guilt and at the same time to see no hope of mercy – that would be to experience hell on earth. So Joseph the wise physician of souls applies true balm.

Every minister of the gospel must do the same. When souls are wounded to the point of despair he must not continue to thunder forth the demands of the law. He must rather point anxious souls to the healing grace of God. He must present Christ in all his attractive beauty as the Friend of sinners and as the refuge of all who flee to him from the terrors of God's law.

It may be that you, dear reader, have a deep sense of your sinfulness before God. You see no hope of mercy, believing yourself too bad to be saved. The Lord Jesus does not accept your verdict on yourself. For such as you he issues a marvellous invitation: 'Come to me, all you who are weary and burdened, and I will give you rest' (*Matt.* 11:28).

Jesus makes no limitation. He does not for a moment allow that your burden of sin is too great for Him to bear. Nor will He deny you rest because of the enormity of your sins. His invitation to you is plain. You are to come to Him as you are with your burden and give it to Him.

The following lines press home his invitation to you:

> *Come, ye weary, heavy-laden,*
> *Lost and ruined by the Fall;*
> *If you wait until you're better,*
> *You will never come at all.*
> *Not the righteous –*
> *Sinners, Jesus came to call.*
>
> Joseph Hart

Secondly, Joseph comforts his brothers from the providence of God, but not in such a way as to excuse their sin. 'I am Joseph your brother, whom ye sold into Egypt' (verse 4, AV), he declares.

Nothing can undo that fact. Joseph was in Egypt because, out of jealousy and malice, they had sold him into slavery there. He does not comfort his brothers by implying in any way that their sin is excused because of the providential good that resulted from their act. Their personal responsibility before God is not diminished at all. Joseph points this out even more forcibly in Genesis 50:20: 'But as for you, ye thought evil against me; but God meant it unto good' (AV).

Joseph comforts his brothers, not by excusing their sin, but by showing them that human sinfulness cannot defeat the gracious purpose of God. He tells them that 'it was to save lives that God sent me ahead of you . . . to preserve for you a remnant on earth' (verses 5 and 7). God will have 'a remnant on earth', a chosen people from whom will come the Saviour of all peoples (*Gen.* 12:3; *Gal.* 3:8; *Rev.* 7:9–10). Human sin will do its worst to Him, but God's gracious, saving purpose will be victorious (*Acts* 2:23–24).

Here is comfort indeed. Without excusing his brothers' sin, Joseph shows them that, in spite of themselves, they were serving the purpose of God. Calvin's comment is apt: 'Joseph was a skilful interpreter of the providence of God, when he borrowed from it an argument for granting forgiveness to his brethren.'[1]

Perhaps the last word should lie with the Apostle Paul, for the story of Joseph marvellously illustrates the great truth that 'where sin abounded, grace did much more abound' (*Rom.* 5:20, AV). God's grace is ultimately invincible.

---

[1] *Commentary on Genesis*, English translation, 1847; reprinted London: Banner of Truth, 1965 (2 volumes in one), vol. 2, p. 380.

# 7

# Preserver and
# Provider

Pharaoh had given Joseph an Egyptian name, Zaphenath-
paneah, and an Egyptian wife, Asenath, daughter of
Potiphera, priest of On (*Gen.* 41:45). In this situation there
must have been considerable pressure on Joseph to assimilate
to Egyptian religion and culture. Perhaps he did to a certain
extent, but the reference to his divining cup (*Gen.* 44:5) may
not be especially significant in this connection. As Gordon
Wenham points out, it may be 'just a threatening comment to
stress the gravity of the offence and to explain why he is sure
the brothers are guilty'.[1]

Though he had an Egyptian name and an Egyptian wife
Joseph kept his identity as a Hebrew, a member of the
covenant people of God. His two sons, Manasseh and
Ephraim, were given not Egyptian but Hebrew names (*Gen.*
41:51–52). Both of the names express Joseph's thankfulness
to God for making him 'forget all his trouble' and for making

---

[1] *Genesis*, Word Biblical Commentary, Vol. 2 (1994), p. 424.

him 'fruitful' in the land of his suffering. Both names also recall the promise 'I am with you' (*Gen.* 39:2–6, 21–23). So, through the names he gave his sons, Joseph expressed his conviction that God had been with him and blessed him.

Because Joseph preserved his identity as a member of God's covenant people, he is able now to be the preserver of those people.

## 1. PRESERVER

Joseph had a whole clan to preserve – some seventy souls (*Gen.* 46:27). He clearly had his eye on the land of Goshen (verse 28) as a suitable place in which they could settle and thrive. Pharaoh himself recognized that it was 'the best part of the land' (*Gen.* 47:6). It also had the advantage that it was in a border area where the Israelites would not be so exposed to the Egyptian way of life. What a reward Joseph's brothers had! They sold him into slavery, and now they were to live on the best land of Egypt.

Joseph wisely advised his brothers to make no secret of who they were. 'When Pharaoh calls you in and asks, "What is your occupation?" you should answer, "Your servants have tended livestock from our boyhood on just as our fathers did." Then you will be allowed to settle in the region of Goshen, for all shepherds are detestable to the Egyptians' (*Gen.* 46:33–34). Pharaoh, for his part, gladly agreed that Joseph's family should be allowed to settle in Goshen (*Gen.* 47:6).

The reason why the Egyptians had such an aversion to shepherds is not stated. They had an aversion to eating with foreigners (*Gen.* 43:32), and their aversion to shepherds was probably based on a deep distrust and fear of nomadic peoples on the part of settled city dwellers, much as gypsies and hippies are shunned today. What is clear, however, is that Joseph turned the aversion of the Egyptians to the advantage of his family. Though some of his brothers would be employed as royal stockmen to take care of Pharaoh's vast herds (verse 6), their occupation served to prevent them losing their identity. They could live apart from the Egyptians in a fertile area in which their numbers would greatly increase.

Had Joseph followed the wisdom of this world, he might have advised his brothers to conceal their occupation – though 'their flocks and herds' (*Gen.* 46:32) would have destroyed any attempt at concealment! But Joseph was moved by godly wisdom – wisdom that resulted in the preservation of the covenant identity of his family. They may have been regarded as detestable to the Egyptians yet, as Calvin observes, 'This ignominy with which they were branded was most profitable to themselves. For, had they been mingled with the Egyptians, they might have been scattered far and wide, but now, seeing that they are objects of detestation, and are thought unworthy to be admitted to common society, they learn, in this state of separation from others, to cherish more fervently mutual union between themselves; and thus the body of the Church, which God had set apart from the whole world, is not dispersed.'[1]

The calling of the church in every generation is to be the people of God, separate and distinct from any particular society in which they are set. The church is not to be conformed 'to the pattern of this world' (*Rom.* 12:2) but to live a distinctive existence, shining 'like stars in the universe' (*Phil.* 2:15), as she holds out the word of life (verse 16).

---

[1] *Commentary on Genesis*, London: Banner of Truth, 1965 (2 volumes in one), vol. 2, p. 395.

It was because the children of Israel preserved their identity in Goshen, even as they greatly increased in numbers there, that Moses and Aaron were able to demand of another Pharaoh, 'This is what the LORD, the God of Israel, says: "Let my people go, so that they may hold a festival to me in the desert"' (*Exod.* 5:1).

## 2. PROVIDER

In Genesis 47:12 a key verb occurs, a verb that will be repeated on the lips of Joseph after the death of Jacob (see *Gen.* 50:21). It is the verb *provide*. In the rest of the chapter Joseph not only assumes the role of provider for his family, but also for the population of Egypt and Canaan (verses 13 and 15) as well.

The effect of the famine, against which Joseph had laid up huge stores of grain (*Gen.* 41:49), is described in three stages. First of all, the Egyptians exchange money (that is, silver) for food (verses 13–14). Joseph brought the money into Pharaoh's palace, a fact which suggests to Calvin how honest he was. 'We know how few persons can touch the money of kings without defiling themselves by peculation'[1] – a comment of great contemporary relevance in the light of widespread governmental corruption in Africa and elsewhere. Calvin aptly observes of Joseph: 'It was a rare and unparalleled integrity, to keep the hands pure amidst such heaps of gold.'[2]

The second stage of the famine begins when 'the money of the people of Egypt and Canaan was gone' (verse 15). Then the Egyptians mortgaged their herds for grain (verses 15–17).

---

[1] *ibid.*, p. 407.     [2] *ibid.*

This is a very significant step, since, in agricultural societies animals are an important capital asset. (For example, in rural Africa wealth is reckoned by the numbers of cattle one owns.)

Joseph must have stored up a great supply of feedstuff to be able to take into Pharaoh's possession the people's 'horses . . . sheep . . . goats and donkeys' (verse 17). Clearly the livestock was not allowed to die of hunger but was exchanged for food (verse 16).

When the famine becomes yet more severe (verse 20), the third stage was reached (verses 18–26). The Egyptians come to Joseph and declare their willingness to mortgage their land and become royal slaves for grain. Their plight is desperate, as they recognize – 'There is nothing left for our lord except our bodies and our land' (verse 18). So they propose a radical measure: 'Buy us and our land in exchange for food, and we with our land will be in bondage to Pharaoh' (verse 19). Joseph acceded to their request. He bought their land on behalf of Pharaoh and made them royal serfs. The NIV's rendering, 'reduced the people to servitude' (verse 21), is unduly strong, for now their food was Pharaoh's responsibility, for which the Egyptians express their gratitude (verse 25).

In interpreting the biblical text at this point we must avoid reading into it the horrors of the African slave trade. If we do, it is impossible to understand the Egyptians' gratitude. What should be appreciated is that, in ancient societies, slavery was the accepted way of bailing out the destitute. Nor need the experience of slavery be harsh. Under a benevolent master like Potiphar, Joseph enjoyed quite a comfortable existence. The law allows that some temporary slaves may elect to become permanent slaves because they love their master (*Exod.* 21:5–6; see also *Deut.* 15:12–17).

Gordon Wenham suggests that 'Ancient slavery at its best was like tenured employment, whereas the free man was more like someone who is self-employed'.[1] Such 'slavery' is not unknown today. In the mid-1970s, a white Christian doctor friend of mine worked for a time in the very poor Ciskei region of South Africa. He and his wife were approached by Patrick, an African teenager, who offered to work for them in return for his food. They agreed to help him. Needless to say he was not 'reduced to servitude'!

The land that the Egyptians surrendered 'became Pharaoh's' (verse 20) and, in exchange, they were given grain to eat and to sow (verse 23). When they reaped the next and subsequent harvests the Egyptians were to contribute one-fifth of the crop to Pharaoh. By contemporary standards this was not a burdensome arrangement. A tax of about twenty per cent would be considered normal. In private business agreements, interest rates could be considerably higher. According to Von Rad, 'in the Babylonian economy the interest rates for the purchase of seed corn went as high as 40 per cent'.[2]

Joseph's measures served two purposes. First, they strengthened the position of Pharaoh and increased his wealth. All the land of Egypt, except that owned by the priests, belonged to Pharaoh, and a fifth of the harvest was his as well (verse 26). This situation continued to the time of the writing of Genesis (and no doubt beyond) – the law established by Joseph is 'still in force today', says the author of Genesis.

---

[1] *Genesis*, p. 449.

[2] Gerhard Von Rad, *Genesis – A Commentary*, 3rd edition, London: SCM Press, 1972, p. 411.

The second purpose served by Joseph's measures is pregnantly stated in verse 27: 'Now the Israelites settled in Egypt in the region of Goshen. They acquired property there and were fruitful and increased greatly in number.' Joseph, of course, did not live to see the full extent of this increase, nor the fear that it produced in the heart of a future Pharaoh. But, had he not been the preserver of his family, there would have been no increase in numbers, no slavery, no Exodus (see *Heb*. 11:22).

There is no mention of the name of God in this chapter. The focus is on Joseph. God seems out of the picture altogether. But He is not. Though hidden, He is, through Joseph, working His purposes out. Secular historians may employ what they term 'methodological atheism', because all they can see are men and movements. They mistake the *hiddenness* of God for the *absence* of God. The Bible never does.

Joseph exemplifies what the Apostle Paul calls all believers to do: 'As we have opportunity, let us do good to all people, especially to those who belong to the family of believers' (*Gal*. 6:10). Joseph used his God-given opportunity to do good, not only to his own family, but also to the inhabitants of Egypt and Canaan. In our 'global village' we have opportunities created for us by the operation of God's providence.

They are unlikely to be as great as Joseph's, but if we are spiritually alert we will be able to seize them and do good. It may be no more than to give 'a cup of cold water' to one of Christ's disciples (*Matt*. 10:42), or an encouraging word to a discouraged believer, but it will do good. And in a suffering, hungry world we can help to alleviate suffering and relieve hunger.

Joseph also models what may be termed *consistent integrity*. He was in a position to enrich himself at Pharaoh's expense, but he refused to do so. Pharaoh could trust him with great power, knowing that Joseph would not abuse it. Whatever our station in life, it should be every believer's aim to be a person of consistent integrity who is not spoiled by advancement nor captivated by power. A Christian should, by definition, be trustworthy and consistently incorruptible.

Some years ago I spoke to a land agent from Northamptonshire. I asked him whether he had known Claude Clarke, my spiritual father, by then deceased, who had once managed a huge estate in rural Northamptonshire. He replied that he had, and then added – with considerable feeling – 'He was a great man.' So was Joseph. What a way to be remembered!

# 8

# Three Great Truths

As his story unfolds, Joseph makes two memorable confessions of faith (*Gen.* 45:5–7; 50:20). Both of them were made at very significant points. The first was made when he revealed his true identity to his brothers (*Gen.* 45:4). When they heard him say, 'I am your brother Joseph, the one you sold into Egypt!' they were terrified. They were thoroughly alarmed because the powerful overlord of Egypt turned out to be the brother they had wronged by selling him into slavery in Egypt.

Joseph's brothers knew that they were completely in his power. They fully expected him to take his revenge upon them. At worst, he could have them executed. At best, he could send them away with nothing in their bags.

Joseph assures his brothers that he will not take vengeance upon them. To their amazement he tells them not to be distressed or angry with themselves for selling him into slavery (verse 5). Like those who crucified our Lord, his brothers acted in ignorance when they sold him into Egypt – ignorance of God's hidden purpose of blessing. God, Joseph assures them, sent him on ahead of them to save lives (verse 5).

Joseph draws the conclusion that enables him to forgive his brothers and to persuade them that he has no intention of visiting his revenge upon them. 'It was not you who sent me here, but God', he says (verse 8). His first confession brings hope to his brothers – hope of his mercy towards them.

It was vital that Joseph's first confession should bring his brothers hope, for otherwise their accusing consciences might well have destroyed them. That they were being troubled by a sense of guilt is clear from what they say to each other after they have had a taste of prison, 'Surely we are being punished because of our brother. We saw how distressed he was when he pleaded with us for his life, but we would not listen; that's why this distress has come upon us' (*Gen.* 42:21).

A conscience that is deeply alarmed by a profound sense of guilt and that is without any hope of mercy is a terrifying accuser. More than that it is a destroyer – you cannot live with it. Therefore, from his understanding of God's providence, Joseph, without excusing their sin, shows his brothers that they were serving the gracious purpose of God in spite of themselves.

The second confession of faith that Joseph made was uttered at another significant point in his relationship with his brothers. Their father Jacob had just died (*Gen.* 49:33). Before he died he left instructions to be passed on to Joseph: 'This is what you are to say to Joseph: "I ask you to forgive your brothers the sins and the wrongs they have committed in treating you so badly." Now please forgive the sins of the servants of the God of your father' (*Gen.* 50:17).

Jacob seems to have envisaged the possibility that, after his death, Joseph might at last take his revenge upon his

[74]

brothers. Certainly Joseph's brothers feared that this would happen (verse 15). Though Joseph had long since forgiven them, they had this nagging doubt: Had he really forgiven them? Supposing, they thought, he has only restrained himself from paying us back as long as our father was alive? What now, when he is dead? Might not the gloves be off?

It is significant that they sent a messenger to Joseph (verse 16), rather than coming to him in person. This suggests that they were in real doubt about what his reaction would be. They need not have been, for 'when their message came to him, Joseph wept' (verse 17).

When his brothers came before Joseph they 'threw themselves down before him' and declared, 'We are your slaves.' In his reply to them Joseph again draws upon his understanding of God's providence. 'Don't be afraid', he said. 'Am I in the place of God? You intended to harm me, but God intended it for good to accomplish what is now being done, the saving of many lives' (verses 19–20). He promises to provide for them and for their children (verse 21).

As in his first confession, so in his second, Joseph has a very practical purpose in mind. He wants to assure his brothers that they are really, truly forgiven. Far from doing them harm, he will be responsible for caring for them and their families. So Joseph reassured them and spoke kindly to them.

Joseph saw very clearly that, if God intended the evil actions of his brothers to work even for their good, he could not possibly act with malice against them. To do so would be to contradict God's gracious purpose and to sin against Him. In particular, it would be to usurp His throne. 'Am I in the place of God?' he asked, to which the answer is a clear negative.

Joseph's two confessions of faith – the second will be considered in detail in the final chapter – show us how much the providence of God meant to Joseph. He obviously had meditated a great deal on the operation of God's providence in his own life and that of his family. For Joseph it was not some purely theoretical doctrine, confessed as one item in a creed, but not of practical relevance in the hurly burly of life. Joseph did not philosophize about God's providence – he dwelt in it, and he 'used' it. For at these two critical points – when he first revealed himself to his brothers and after the death of Jacob – Joseph used the doctrine of God's providence to calm and reassure his brothers.

We would do well to imitate Joseph at this point. We should dwell much upon the doctrine of God's providence. It should be the subject of careful meditation, leading us to bow before its mystery and to adore God's particular care for us and our families. If we learn to live in God's providence, we shall be better prepared to react in a godly way when afflictions come our way. Then we may even be able to say with Job, 'Though he slay me, yet will I trust in him' (*Job* 13:15, AV).

Wrapped up in Joseph's first confession are several truths that relate to God's providence. The first is that it is all-inclusive.

## 1. God's Providence Is All-Inclusive

By *all-inclusive*, I mean that God's providence includes the sinful acts of men and women. Joseph recognizes this when he says, 'I am your brother Joseph, the one you sold into Egypt.' In no way does Joseph exculpate his brothers. Their intention was purely evil. They acted out of hatred, not caring what happened to their brother. 'You intended to harm me', he declares (*Gen.* 50:20).

Men and women may have only an evil intention in their hearts. They have no thought of serving God's purposes in what they plot and do. Yet in spite of themselves – and in spite of their sin – they serve the hidden purpose of God. This was the case with Joseph's brothers. They hated him because he was their father's favourite. They seized the opportunity to be rid of him. They consigned him to an unknown fate. They deceived their father for years, pretending that Joseph was dead.

What a catalogue of collective wickedness! Yet, though he fully recognizes the evil of what they had done to him, Joseph is able to say that in selling him into slavery in Egypt they were fulfilling God's purpose – 'It was to save lives that God sent me ahead of you' (*Gen.* 45:5). God raised up Joseph – 'He made me father to Pharaoh, lord of his entire household and ruler of all Egypt' (verse 8) – so that he could use his power to save his family from extinction.

The truth that the providence of God includes within it the sinful acts of men and women runs throughout Scripture. I give two examples out of many. In the year that our Lord was crucified, Caiaphas was high priest in Jerusalem. Being a politically inclined priest – representative of a breed still with us – he was afraid that the Roman rulers might regard the Jesus movement as a threat to the stability of the country, with the result that the whole nation would be made to suffer for its existence. So Caiaphas cynically put forward the idea that it was better to get rid of Jesus than to have the wrath of the Romans descend upon the entire people. Said Caiaphas, 'It is better for you that one man die for the people than that the whole nation perish' (*John* 11:50).

So far as Caiaphas' own intention was concerned, he spoke as a cynical, worldly high priest. But he spoke truer than he knew, for 'he prophesied that Jesus would die for the Jewish nation, and not only for that nation but also for the scattered children of God, to bring them together and make them one' (verses 51–52). In wanting to be rid of Jesus, Caiaphas was serving the hidden purpose of God, for in the deepest sense it was expedient that Jesus should die.

A second example is found in Peter's address to the crowd on the day of Pentecost. As he pressed home the wickedness of what they had done to Jesus, he said, 'You, with the help of wicked men, put him to death by nailing him to the cross' (Acts 2:23). Yet what they did was not outside the sovereign purpose of God. Immediately before the words just quoted Peter declared, 'This man was handed over to you by God's set purpose and foreknowledge.' The crucifixion of the Lord Jesus was decreed by God the Father from all eternity, but the wicked hands of men brought it about when they nailed the Saviour to the cross.

Two objections are brought against the truth that God's providence includes the sinful acts of men and women.

The first objection is, *Does not this make God the Author of sin?* How, some ask, can God use the sinful acts of human beings without being directly responsible for them? How can the charge be avoided that His all-inclusive sovereignty makes Him the Author of sin?

When we consider the working of God's providence, we are confronted by mystery. This is why John Flavel's great work on the subject is entitled *The Mystery of Providence*.[1]

---

[1] Flavel, *Divine Conduct, or, The Mystery of Providence*, 1678; reprinted London: Banner of Truth, 1963. Also in *The Works of John Flavel*, 6 volumes, 1820; reprinted London: Banner of Truth, 1968, vol. 4.

Just how God uses the sinful acts of men without sharing in their sin is a mystery to us. Yet, if 'God's sovereignty means He does what He wants to do, when He wants to do it, and without having to give an explanation for why He did it'[1], how could it be otherwise?

When God uses the sinful acts of men and women, He in no way compromises his holiness – He is as holy as He ever has been or ever will be. Likewise when He includes evil acts within His purposes, He is always sovereign. As Augustine wrote, 'Nothing therefore happens unless the Omnipotent wills it to happen. He either permits it to happen, or He brings it about Himself.'[2] Calvin's observation is very much to the point, 'But God works wonderfully through their means [that is, through the actions of evil men], in order that, from their impurity He may bring forth His perfect righteousness.'[3]

Because mystery attaches to the operations of God's providence, it is not surprising that objections should arise in the minds of carnal people who are not prepared to live with mystery. Such are not willing to accept that there are limits to reason, beyond which it is not possible to go. For the believer, facing the mystery of God's providence, the right approach is to realize that God is God. He is so far above us that much of His doing is hidden from us. 'Clouds and thick darkness surround him' (*Psa.* 97:2) – such is the hiddenness of God. But, as the verse continues, 'righteousness and

---

[1] Roger Ellsworth, 'Pastoral benefits of the sovereignty of God', *The Founders Journal*, Issue 51, Winter 2003, p. 13. This article is also on the Banner of Truth website, www.banneroftruth.co.uk

[2] Augustine, *Enchiridion on Faith, Hope and Love*, ch. 24, para. 95, quoted by Ellsworth in the article just cited.

[3] Calvin, *Commentary on Genesis*, vol. 2, p. 378.

justice are the foundation of his throne'. Mystery does not hide righteousness and justice. 'God is light: in him there is no darkness at all' (1 John 1:5).

Joseph's brothers meant only evil when they sold him into slavery, yet God meant what they did for good. It might appear at first sight that God, in using their sinful action, is somehow contaminated by so doing. However, there is a wide gulf between what Joseph's brothers purposed and what God purposed. They purposed Joseph's disappearance, out of hatred; God planned to preserve the whole family, out of love. They intended nothing but evil; God intended nothing but good.

It is this wide gulf that removes God altogether from the evil of their hearts. This is always the case when God's providence embraces the evil acts of men. His using of evil men in no way contaminates Him. He brings forth good, and He is in no way an accomplice in their sins. His 'eyes are too pure to look on evil', and he 'cannot tolerate wrong' (Hab. 1:13).

The second objection that is brought against the biblical doctrine of providence is this, *If God includes the sinful acts of men in the workings of his providence are they not provided with an excuse for their sin?*

Could not the brothers of Joseph have argued that they were free from guilt because what they did turned out for good? They could, perhaps, but they did not. They acknowledged the sinfulness of what they had done to Joseph. They confessed to each other, 'We saw how distressed he was when he pleaded with us for his life, but we would not listen; that's why this distress has come upon us' (Gen. 42:21). Lest there be any doubt about the matter Reuben pinpointed the issue, 'Didn't I tell you not to sin against the boy? But you wouldn't listen! Now we must give an accounting for his blood' (verse 22).

Joseph's brothers recognized that they were personally responsible for what they had done. They meant evil – and they knew it! That is why they were afraid. They make no attempt to excuse their action because it turned out for good. So we must never argue that, because 'in all things God works for the good of those who love him' (*Rom.* 8:28), we have no personal responsibility for our sins. If God should overrule our sin and folly for our good, we are not thereby absolved from responsibility and the need for repentance. We are bound to give God thanks, but we dare not offer excuses for our sins.

Our responsibility as Christians is to keep our eyes on our duty – what God requires of us. Then we shall acknowledge that there is much that we do not perform. There are commandments that we do not keep. Though God may be pleased to overrule our sins for good, our concern must be with our duty to God rather than the providential outcome. The wonderful ways of God in providence are never meant to give us licence to sin, or to provide us with an excuse for sinning.

We can marvel at God's ways but we must never, never use them as a 'get-out' from the acknowledgement of our personal responsibility before him.

The child of David and Bathsheba was Solomon, who was famed for his wisdom. But the outcome of their union in no way excuses David's sin (see *Psa.* 51:2–3). We should never allow the thought that the good outcome of a chain of events may serve as an excuse for human sin. The outcome of Joseph being sold into Egypt was good – eventually – but his brothers had no excuse for what they did.

God holds us personally responsible for our sins. It is therefore sheer wickedness on our part to attempt to clear ourselves of blame by pointing to a good outcome. With David we must refuse to justify ourselves, but confess with heartfelt sorrow: 'Against you, you only, have I sinned and done what is evil in your sight, so that you are proved right when you speak and justified when you judge' (*Psa.* 51:4).

## 2. GOD'S PROVIDENCE LOOKS A GREAT WAY FORWARD

When Joseph made his first confession to his brothers he bore testimony to a second great truth – how far forward God's providence reached. He was seventeen when they sold him into Egypt (*Gen.* 37:2). He was thirty years old when he was elevated to the throne next to Pharaoh (*Gen.* 41:46). Seven years of plenty had elapsed, and already two years of famine (*Gen.* 45:6). So Joseph was sold into slavery at least twenty-two years before he would be able to save his family from starvation.

God's providence, then, 'looks a great way forward and has a long reach'.[1] Joseph came to understand the meaning of what had happened to him – sold into Egypt and unjustly imprisoned, elevated to a position of great authority – long after these events unfolded. Yet even he did not realize how far forward God's providence reached. He seems to have seen the sojourn of his family in Egypt as a temporary measure until the famine was past (*Gen.* 45:11). When the five remaining years had gone he expected them to return to Canaan. In fact their stay in Egypt was to be far longer, as God had already made known to Abraham. God spoke to

[1] *Matthew Henry's Commentary*, on Genesis 45.

Abraham in a dream: 'Know for certain that your descendants will be strangers in a country not their own, and they
will be enslaved and ill-treated four hundred years' (*Gen.*
15:13). In Egypt Joseph's clan would greatly multiply in
numbers. They would become 'a great nation there' (*Gen.*
46:3, see also *Exod.* 1:7), in fulfilment of the promise made to
Abraham so long before (*Gen.* 12:2).

How far reaching is the providence of God! It spans
centuries, yet it turns on specific events – the call to
Abraham – the selling of Joseph into Egypt – a terrible
famine. It embraces individuals, for they are not lost in the
maze of history. So there is Abram in Ur, Jacob in Canaan,
Joseph in Egypt.

If God's providence looks so far forward, then how foolish
we are – you and I – to demand of God an instant explanation of what happens to us. When the sudden strokes of His
providence fall upon us, we immediately and instinctively
demand to know why. We want to know what God did not
choose to tell Joseph at the time – why he was sold into Egypt
– why he was unjustly cast into prison.

Joseph could, of course, have given way to unbelief. He
could have said to himself, 'Since I have been sold into Egypt,
and since I cannot understand why, I conclude that my life
has neither meaning nor purpose to it.' How wrong Joseph
would have been, if that had been his attitude – which it
clearly was not. But it is often our attitude. When God's
chastening strokes fall, we immediately demand to know
why, and because heaven is silent we conclude that life has
no purpose to it.

We must beware of the development of such an attitude in
us. Should it appear, we must strongly resist it. We must learn
the wisdom of waiting for the outcome – for God in His time

[83]

to reveal his purpose. Joseph had the wisdom to do this, which is why his confession is so memorable. Sold into slavery so long before, Joseph could now see God's purpose at last – 'it was to save lives that God sent me ahead of you' (*Gen.* 45:5).

Let us cultivate a like wisdom. And if in this life God does not see fit to reveal all of His purposes to us, why should we fret? We believe in heaven, do we not? We believe in eternity. Then surely we can wait – you and I – until we reach the courts above, for God to show us that He does all things well? Then, in realms that are fairer than day, we shall be fully satisfied, and marvel at the wisdom of God. We should think with shame of our demands to know in an instant why God permitted such and such to happen to us. In heaven, on the contrary, our hearts will be full of praise.

> *With mercy and with judgment*
> *My web of time He wove,*
> *And aye the dews of sorrow*
> *Were lustred by His love:*
> *I'll bless the hand that guided,*
> *I'll bless the heart that planned,*
> *When throned where glory dwelleth*
> *In Immanuel's land.*
> Anne Ross Cousin

### 3. GOD'S PROVIDENCE OPERATES FOR THE GOOD OF HIS PEOPLE

A very significant word appears in verse 7, the word *remnant*. The idea of a remnant often occurs in the context of God's gracious purposes. He preserved a remnant from the flood that destroyed humanity – Noah and his family. He called

Abram, so small a remnant that he was but one man. He promised to make of him a great nation, and that all the families of the earth should be blessed through him.

Here, according to Joseph, God is working to preserve a remnant, working to save his covenant people from starvation. What happened to Joseph, though it was painful and distressing at the time, was for the good of God's people. Joseph was not an isolated individual, but a member of God's chosen people. Thus, what befell him was not to be measured solely by its effect upon him.

Now we in our self-centredness have a habitual tendency to measure things solely by how they affect us personally. But if we are Christians, are we not members of Christ's body, the church, and therefore members one of another (*Eph.* 4:25)? Should we not, then, think much less of our own good, our own comfort, than of the good of the church and the furtherance of the gospel?

This is what the apostle Paul did when he was in prison for the sake of Christ. Some of his detractors tried to stir up trouble for him by preaching Christ 'out of envy and rivalry' (*Phil.* 1:15,17). Yet Paul could rejoice because 'whether from false motives or true, Christ is preached' (verse 18). He could think as he did because he thought of himself, not as an isolated individual, but as a member of the body of Christ.

Paul's troubles were many, but he never gave way to self-pity. The reason is not hard to find. He tells the believers in Corinth that God is 'the Father of compassion and the God of all comfort, who comforts us in all our troubles, so that we can comfort those in any trouble with the comfort we ourselves have received from God' (*2 Cor.* 1:3–4). Paul sees the comfort that he received in his troubles as intended not for him alone, but also for the benefit of fellow members of the body of Christ, the church.

You and I need to grasp this truth: God's providence, though it embraces us as individual believers, is never to be isolated from His purpose for *all* his people. When suffering, for example, comes to the individual Christian it is never for him or her alone. In the way that the believer accepts it and 'uses' it, good is brought to God's people. They are comforted and encouraged as they see the grace of God at work in the life of a fellow-believer. They see the sufficiency of God's grace in the life of the sufferer and so are helped to draw on that grace as well.

We must cultivate the habit of thinking of ourselves as members of Christ's body. We must resist any tendency to put ourselves at the centre of God's purposes. As we do so, we shall find that we become more concerned for the good of the church than for our own personal comforts. And self-pity will not then find a place in our hearts.

# 9

# Three More
# Great Truths

Jacob had died and, in accordance with his wish, had been
buried in the land of Canaan, in the cave in the field of
Machpelah, near Mamre, which Abraham had bought as a
burial place (Gen. 50:12). With their father dead and buried,
Joseph's brothers became very frightened. They feared that,
without Jacob's restraining influence, Joseph would exact his
revenge. This is how they (wrongly) perceived their situation:
'When Joseph's brothers saw that their father was dead, they
said, "What if Joseph holds a grudge against us and pays us
back for all the wrongs we did to him?"' (verse 15). They
clearly were not persuaded that Joseph had completely
forgiven them.They feared that he would now take his
revenge, which they expected to be swift and terrible.

Joseph, then, must now reassure them. He must persuade
them that their fears are not justified. Again he points them
to the providence of God which, as he understands it, rules
out any thought of revenge. In the school of God's

providence, according to the words of his confession (verse 19–20), Joseph had learned three great truths. It was these that enabled him to forgive and reassure his brothers (verse 21).

## 1. THE RIGHTING OF WRONGS

The first lesson was to leave all the righting of his wrongs to God. As we have seen, Joseph's brothers were afraid that Joseph would now pay them back for all the wrongs they had done to him. Some commentators suggest that they therefore made up a story about Jacob's dying wish. They sent word to Joseph, purporting to express their father's desire: 'Your father left these instructions before he died, "This is what you are to say to Joseph: I ask you to forgive your brothers the sins and wrongs they committed in treating you so badly." (verse 17). Other commentators are not convinced. They think that Jacob *did* leave such instructions, because he wanted the brothers to make full confession of their sins – not because he doubted Joseph's willingness to forgive them.

When the message reached Joseph he wept, proving that there was no bitterness in his heart towards them. For their part, his brothers showed the depth of their repentance by putting themselves absolutely at Joseph's disposal as his slaves (verse 18). They gave Joseph a blank cheque, as it were, to do with them as he pleased, much as the prodigal son did when he returned home to his father (*Luke* 15:19).

How did Joseph reply to his brothers? He told them not to be afraid, and then he asked them, 'Am I in the place of God?' (verse 19). In effect, Joseph is saying that it is not for him to usurp God's throne: 'It is not for me to act as your judge and to visit vengeance upon you. That is God's work, not mine.'

It is clear that Joseph had been taught by providence to rest his cause with God – to wait for Him to right the wrongs done to him. Great wrong had been done to him when Potiphar's wife had falsely accused him of violating her, and her husband, believing her story, had had Joseph cast into prison. But God had vindicated him when he was taken out of prison and raised to a throne next to Pharaoh's. How marvellously God vindicated Joseph in a way that would never have occurred to him, had he tried to vindicate himself. So, taught by God, Joseph is able to put his brothers' fears to rest. He will not take it out on them for what they had done to him so many years before.

Joseph had no bitterness in his heart against them for he had learned to leave the righting of his wrongs to God. This is a lesson that every believer needs to learn. We need not strive to vindicate ourselves. We are to put our cause in God's hands and to love our enemies, truly forgiving them. At the height of the Downgrade Controversy, when he was being vilified by many who were once his friends, C. H. Spurgeon said, 'I am willing to be eaten of dogs for the next fifty years, but the more distant future will vindicate me.' Like Joseph he had learned to leave the righting of his wrongs to God.

Joseph, though it had not yet been made known, was acting according to the teaching of the law of Moses, 'Do not seek revenge or bear a grudge against one of your people, but love your neighbour as yourself, I am the LORD' (*Lev.* 19:18). God will, in perfect justice, vindicate His people. He declares, 'It is mine to avenge. I will repay. In due time their foot will slip' (*Deut.* 32:35). Therefore believers are able to wait, and not to be disturbed when wrong is done to them. What wisdom there is in Proverbs 20:22, 'Do not say, "I'll pay you back for this wrong." Wait for the LORD and he will deliver you.'

In his treatment of his brothers, Joseph marvellously anticipates the Lord Jesus Christ who 'when he suffered . . . made no threats. Instead he entrusted himself to him who judges justly' (1 Pet. 2:23). He also illustrates Paul's teaching in Romans 12:19: 'Do not take revenge but leave room for God's wrath, for it is written: "It is mine to avenge; I will repay", says the Lord.'

When wrong is done to you, have you learned from the working of God's providence to leave its righting to God? You may safely do so for two reasons. First, *He is perfectly just.* His punishment will exactly fit the sin committed. He will be neither too lenient nor too severe, whereas we may be either, though we are more likely to err on the side of severity. If we have a bitter spirit within us, if we have a deep, well-nursed grudge for wrong done to us, we shall very likely pay back double what we have received!

A second reason why we can safely leave the righting of our wrongs to God is that *He knows all the facts.* We do not, but God does, and so the execution of His justice is always based upon His perfect knowledge. Therefore we are not to play God. We are not to trespass on His prerogative. We are to follow the counsel of Georg Neumark (1621–81):

> *Leave God to order all thy ways*
> *And hope in Him whate'er betide;*
> *Thou'lt find Him in the evil days*
> *Thy all-sufficient strength and guide.*
> *Who trusts in God's unchanging love*
> *Builds on the Rock that nought can move.*

How blessed we are in leaving the righting of our wrongs to God. Resigning them to God's justice takes away bitterness from our souls. We are saved from fretfulness and kept calm. Have we learned to commit ourselves to God – to leave our vindication in His hands? Or do we harbour grudges, sometimes for years? Do we wait for the chance to get even – and more than even? If we do, then we are forgetting who we are and who God is. 'Those that avenge themselves step into the place of God' (Matthew Henry), which is sheer folly.

## 2. GOD'S HAND, EVEN IN MAN'S MALICE

Joseph, according to his own confession, had learned a second great truth: 'You intended to harm me, but God intended it for good' (verse 20), he declared.

What a deep lesson this is! It is not a lesson learned by the natural man who is devoid of the Spirit of God. For he estimates the value of everything in terms of the pleasure it either gives him or denies him. Therefore if something happens that gives him pleasure – if it serves his creature comfort – then it is good. F or he defines good always in terms of what gives him pleasure. But if something evil happens – if he suffers loss or pain – then he cannot see how good can come from it in any way. So he reacts, sometimes to the extreme of cursing God (see Job 2:9).

Many a Christian also fails to learn this lesson. Too many Christians have been taught that the Christian life is a bed of roses. 'Trust Christ, and your troubles will be at an end' summarizes the message they have received. So when troubles come, as our Lord warned that they would (*John* 15:18–21), they are knocked flat. They become despondent because they feel that God has let them down, when all that He has done is to allow their foolish expectations to be shattered.

Joseph was spared such despondency because he had learned the great truth that, even in the malice men show to God's servants, God has a good and gracious purpose. It was a thoroughly evil act that his brothers were guilty of when they sold Joseph into slavery. There was not a trace of pity or compassion in it (see Genesis 42:21). They shut their ears to Joseph's pleas for mercy and deceived their father for years, adding to his sorrow at losing his favourite wife the sorrow of losing his favourite son. Yet God uses their evil act to deliver them from death. In God's plan what they did to Joseph worked for their good and the good of their families. This outcome did not come about because of any traces of good in them or in their deed, but because God meant it for good.

Joseph was able to forgive his brothers and to provide for them and their families (verse 21) because he had learned to see God's hand even in their malice. If he can see the good that God has wrought, then he can find it in his heart to forgive them.

The Bible consistently teaches us that the malicious acts that men do cannot overcome God's good and gracious purposes. We see this supremely in the crucifixion of our Lord. Those who plotted to kill Him gave Him a farce of a trial, mocked and scourged Him, and finally had Him nailed to a cross intended only evil (*Acts* 2:23). But God meant it for good. And what good! The good that He promised long ago to Abraham – that in him all the families of the earth would be blessed (*Gen.* 12:13). Through the evil acts of rejection and crucifixion come amazing blessings – the forgiveness of sins, adoption into God's family, the gift of the Holy Spirit, and the glories of the new creation. Such evil – to crucify the Lord of glory! Such good – salvation for a great multitude that no man can number (*Rev.* 7:9)!

As Christians we can plainly see the good that God intended when evil men crucified His Son. The problem is that so often we cannot see God's hand in the evil that men and women do to us personally. We can see it in what men did to Jesus, but not to ourselves. Yet Romans 8:28 is still in the Bible, so we believe it and apply it, as C. H. Spurgeon did in his early days in London when many were bitter in their criticisms of his preaching. 'Mine enemies', he said, 'have done me real good.'

Does a friend forsake you? The experience will do you real good if it drives you closer to God. Does a disappointment befall you? Then it will be a blessing if you realize that God will never disappoint His own. Does a hurt come to you? It will do you good if it makes you look to heaven where there is no pain. Are your comforts taken away? It is that God may teach you that He is more concerned to see you holy than comfortable.

Keep on learning this truth, that God brings good out of men's malice, for we so often forget it when we most need to remember it – in the buffets we receive and the disappoint - ments we experience.

Paulus Gerhardt (1607–76) points us in the right direction:

> *Thou on the Lord rely,*
> *So safe shalt thou go on;*
> *Fix on His work thy steadfast eye,*
> *So shall thy work be done.*

> *No profit canst thou gain*
> *By self-consuming care;*
> *To Him commend thy cause; His ear*
> *Attends the softest prayer.*

*Thy everlasting truth,*
  *Father, Thy ceaseless love,*
*Sees all Thy children's wants, and knows*
  *What best for each will prove.*

*Thou everywhere hast sway*
  *And all things serve Thy might;*
*Thy every act pure blessing is,*
  *Thy path unsullied light.*

(Translated by John Wesley, 1703–91)

## 3. REPAYING EVIL WITH PRACTICAL LOVE

Joseph learned another lesson from the working of God's providence. Providence had dealt kindly with him, though his brothers had done him ill. So, like providence, he will do them good. 'Don't be afraid,' he says, 'I will provide for you and your children' (verse 21).

How blessed it is to be taught by God's providence to repay evil with practical love! In this Joseph anticipates both our Lord's example and His teaching. For those who crucified Him He entreats the forgiveness of His Father (*Luke* 23:34). He healed the ear of one of the group that came to arrest Him (*Luke* 22:50–51). And when He was reviled, He reviled not again (*1 Pet.* 2:23, AV).

Our Lord taught His disciples to love their enemies and to pray for them (*Matt.* 5:44). And so did His apostles. The apostle Paul, quoting Proverbs 25:20–21, urges the believers in Rome not to repay anyone evil for evil (*Rom.* 12:17), but rather, 'if your enemy is hungry feed him; if he is thirsty, give him something to drink. In doing this, you will heap burning coals on his head. Do not be overcome by evil, but overcome evil with good.'

To repay evil with practical love – this is real Christianity. Sadly, it is rare, far too rare, for far too many Christians repay evil with evil. They bear grudges and settle scores, thus demonstrating that Joseph was much more of a 'Christian' than they. What of you? What of me? Are we like Joseph? Are we like our Lord? Are we real Christians, or Christians in name only – self-called Christians or the genuine article?

Looking back over the life of Joseph surely prompts us to put some searching questions to ourselves. Have we learned to live in God's providence, to bow to it, to accept it, to draw comfort from it? Do we 'trust God when providence seems to run quite contrary to promises' (Thomas Watson)?

The providence of God in the life of Joseph is the providence of our God today. It is no different now from what it was then – for He is the same God. So we may confidently rest in providence. 'Your bread is in its cupboard, your money is in its purse, your safety in its enfolding arms' (John Flavel).

What more could we want? What more do we need?

# MYSTERIOUS WAYS

# The Mystery of Providence

## JOHN FLAVEL

Do we believe that everything in the world and in our own lives down to the minutest details is ordered by the providence of God? Do we ever take time to observe and meditate on the workings of providence?

As the Puritan John Flavel (1628–91) shows in this famous work, it should be a delight to us to discern how God works all things in the world for His own glory and His people's good, but an even greater pleasure to observe the particular designs of providence in our own lives. 'Oh, what a world of rarities', says Flavel, 'are to be found in providence . . . With what profound wisdom, infinite tenderness and incessant vigilance it has managed all that concerns us from first to last.'

It was to persuade Christians of the excellence of observing and meditating on providence that Flavel first published this book, based on the words 'God that performeth all things for me' (*Psa.* 57:2), in 1678. Since then it has enriched the Christian lives of very many.

'My life seemed like a jigsaw of many pieces. It was not until I read John Flavel's *The Mystery of Providence* (Banner of Truth) that I realized there was a divine purpose holding every part together and providing the plan.'

Derek Eagles, in EVANGELICAL TIMES

ISBN 0 85151 104 X
224 pp., paperback

# Behind a Frowning Providence

## JOHN J. MURRAY

Sorrow and suffering are unavoidable, but they are often so feared that we do not face them or discuss them as we should. This booklet talks openly about these things, and shows why faith is able to triumph in the face of the severest trials because it focuses on the character of God and His promises to His people.

John J. Murray writes out of his years of experience as a Christian minister and counsellor, but he also draws on his own experience of pain and sorrow, bringing a message of encouragement which speaks to both mind and heart.

'A wonderful booklet for afflicted saints.'

NEW HORIZONS

ISBN 0 85151 572 X
32 pp., booklet

*For free illustrated catalogue please write to*

THE BANNER OF TRUTH TRUST

3 Murrayfield Road,
Edinburgh EH12 6EL
UK

P O Box 621, Carlisle,
Philadelphia 17013,
USA